Microsoft®
Outlook® 2000
For Windows®

FOR

DUMMIES®

by Bill Dyszel

Hungry Minds™

HUNGRY MINDS, INC.

New York, NY ◆ Cleveland, OH ◆ Indianapolis, IN

Microsoft® Outlook® 2000 For Windows® For Dummies® Quick Reference

Published by
Hungry Minds, Inc.
909 Third Avenue
New York, NY 10022
www.hungryminds.com

Library of Congress Catalog Card No.: 99-88740

ISBN: 0-7645-0472-X

Printed in the United States of America

10 9 8 7

1O/SZ/QT/QR/IN

Distributed in the United States by Hungry Minds, Inc.

Distributed by CDG Books Canada Inc. for Canada; by Transworld Publishers Limited in the United Kingdom; by IDG Norge Books for Norway; by IDG Sweden Books for Sweden; by IDG Books Australia Publishing Corporation Pty. Ltd. for Australia and New Zealand; by TransQuest Publishers Pte Ltd. for Singapore, Malaysia, Thailand, Indonesia, and Hong Kong; by Gotop Information Inc. for Taiwan; by ICG Muse, Inc. for Japan; by Intersoft for South Africa; by Eyrolles for France; by International Thomson Publishing for Germany, Austria and Switzerland; by Distribuidora Cuspide for Argentina; by LR International for Brazil; by Galileo Libros for Chile; by Ediciones ZETA S.C.R. Ltda. for Peru; by WS Computer Publishing Corporation, Inc., for the Philippines; by Contemporanea de Ediciones for Venezuela; by Express Computer Distributors for the Caribbean and West Indies; by Micronesia Media Distributor, Inc. for Micronesia; by Chips Computadoras S.A. de C.V. for Mexico; by Editorial Norma de Panama S.A. for Panama; by American Bookshops for Finland.

For general information on Hungry Minds' products and services please contact our Customer Care Department within the U.S. at 800-762-2974, outside the U.S. at 317-572-3993 or fax 317-572-4002.

For sales inquiries and reseller information, including discounts, premium and bulk quantity sales, and foreign-language translations, please contact our Customer Care Department at 800-434-3422, fax 317-572-4002, or write to Hungry Minds, Inc., Attn: Customer Care Department, 10475 Crosspoint Boulevard, Indianapolis, IN 46256.

For information on licensing foreign or domestic rights, please contact our Sub-Rights Customer Care Department at 650-653-7098.

For information on using Hungry Minds' products and services in the classroom or for ordering examination copies, please contact our Educational Sales Department at 800-434-2086 or fax 317-572-4005.

Please contact our Public Relations Department at 212-884-5163 for press review copies or 212-884-5000 for author interviews and other publicity information or fax 212-884-5400.

For authorization to photocopy items for corporate, personal, or educational use, please contact Copyright Clearance Center, 222 Rosewood Drive, Danvers, MA 01923, or fax 978-750-4470.

Hungry Minds™ is a trademark of Hungry Minds, Inc.

About the Author

Bill Dyszel writes frequently for leading magazines, including *PC* magazine, *Success* magazine, *Chief Executive* magazine, and *Computer Shopper,* while also working as a consultant to many of New York's leading firms in the securities, advertising, and publishing industries. His list of current and former clients includes Salomon Brothers, First Boston, Goldman Sachs, Ogilvy & Mather, and KPMG Peat Marwick. An award-winning public speaker, he enjoys entertaining audiences with talks about the pleasures and pitfalls of using modern technology. He is also the author of *PalmPilot For Dummies* (IDG Books Worldwide, Inc.).

The world of high technology has led Mr. Dyszel to grapple with such subjects as multimedia (or how to make your $2,000 computer do the work of a $20 radio), personal information managers (how to make your $3,000 laptop computer do the work of a $3 date book), and graphics programs (how to make your $5,000 package of computers and peripheral devices do the work of a 50-cent box of crayons). All joking aside, he has found that after you figure out the process, most of this stuff can be useful, helpful, and, yes, even cool.

Like many public figures with skeletons in their closets, this author has a secret past. Before entering the computer industry, he sang with the New York City Opera and worked regularly on the New York stage as a singer, actor, and writer in numerous plays, musicals, and operas. His opera spoof — *99% ARTFREE!* — won critical praise from *The New York Times,* New York *Daily News,* and the Associated Press when he performed the show off-Broadway.

Author's Acknowledgments

I'd like to thank all the wonderful people who helped me make this book entertaining and useful to the reader, especially Paul Sanna, Rebecca Whitney, Joyce Pepple, Mary Corder, Mary Bednarek, Diane Steele, and the whole staff of IDG Books Worldwide, who make this series possible.

Publisher's Acknowledgments

We're proud of this book; please send us your comments through our Hungry Minds Online Registration Form located at: www.dummies.com.

Some of the people who helped bring this book to market include the following:

Acquisitions, Editorial, and Media Development

Project Editor: Rebecca Whitney

Acquisitions Editor: Joyce Pepple

Technical Editor: Bill Karow

Editorial Manager: Mary C. Corder

Media Development Manager: Heather Heath Dismore

Editorial Assistant: Paul E. Kuzmic

Special Help

David Mehring, Suzanne Thomas

Production

Project Coordinator: Regina Snyder

Layout and Graphics: Angela F. Hunckler, Chrissie Johnson, Jane E. Martin, Brent Savage, Jacque Schneider, Rashell Smith, Brian Torwelle

Proofreaders: Kelli Botta, Laura Bowman, Joel K. Draper, Nancy Price, Rebecca Senninger, Janet M. Withers

Indexer: Johanna VanHoose

General and Administrative

Hungry Minds, Inc.: John Kilcullen, CEO; Bill Barry, President and COO; John Ball, Executive VP, Operations & Administration; John Harris, CFO

Hungry Minds Technology Publishing Group: Richard Swadley, Senior Vice President and Publisher; Mary Bednarek, Vice President and Publisher, Networking and Certification; Walter R. Bruce III, Vice President and Publisher, General User and Design Professional; Joseph Wikert, Vice President and Publisher, Programming; Mary C. Corder, Editorial Director, Branded Technology Editorial; Andy Cummings, Publishing Director, General User and Design Professional; Barry Pruett, Publishing Director, Visual

Hungry Minds Manufacturing: Ivor Parker, Vice President, Manufacturing

Hungry Minds Marketing: John Helmus, Assistant Vice President, Director of Marketing

Hungry Minds Online Management: Brenda McLaughlin, Executive Vice President, Chief Internet Officer

Hungry Minds Production for Branded Press: Debbie Stailey, Production Director

Hungry Minds Sales: Roland Elgey, Senior Vice President, Sales and Marketing; Michael Violano, Vice President, International Sales and Sub Rights

◆

The publisher would like to give special thanks to Patrick J. McGovern, without whom this book would not have been possible.

◆

Table of Contents

How to Use This Book

Welcome to *Microsoft Outlook 2000 For Windows For Dummies Quick Reference,* the compact, travel-size version of the full-strength *Microsoft Outlook 2000 For Windows For Dummies.*

As they say on *Dragnet,* this book provides "Just the facts, ma'am." I just tell you how to do what you need to do in Outlook and leave out the details about why. For more elaborate explanations of the whys and wherefores of Outlook, check out the companion volume, *Microsoft Outlook 2000 For Windows For Dummies* (published by IDG Books Worldwide, Inc.).

How This Book Is Organized

You won't find out in this one skinny volume everything you need to know about Microsoft Outlook. That's why I wrote a fat, friendly volume called *Microsoft Outlook 2000 For Windows For Dummies*. If you can't decide between this light, lowfat version and the other, authoritative, luxury version, I recommend keeping things simple and getting both. (I like to be helpful.)

This book is organized alphabetically by task so that you can easily find information by browsing through the parts or by looking in the index or table of contents.

Outlook is simple enough to use, and many different tasks are done with the same tools, so you'll probably pick it up pretty quickly. With a little help from this book about where to begin and how to get started, you can find your way without much fuss.

What's in This Book

This book contains seven parts and a glossary.

Part I: All about Outlook

Outlook works differently from some of the other Microsoft programs. Outlook is broken into different modules (Inbox and Contacts, for example), each performing a different function. This book will help you get a tight handle on the different Outlook modules. I also include instructions for using a few of the more interesting — and free! — specialized applications you can access from the Microsoft Web site. I tried them and found using them fun, but frustrating at first. These tips should save you the frustration.

Part II: E-Mail

Using e-mail is quick and easy, and Outlook can make it easier. This part shows you the nitty-gritty details of exchanging messages with individuals or groups and using the Outlook features that make e-mail such an efficient business tool.

Part III: Calendar

If time is money, your calendar should make you rich, right? This part of the book gives you the basic rundown on the tools Outlook offers to help you manage your time; for managing money, however, you're on your own.

Part IV: Tasks

When you do that voodoo that you do so well, you may want to keep a list of things to do (your Voodoo To Do), just to be sure that the things you want to do get done. I show you how to use Outlook for managing your tasks with a minimum of black magic.

Part V: Contacts

If you're exchanging e-mail and keeping a calendar of appointments, I assume that other people are involved. (Otherwise, look for my upcoming book *Microsoft Outlook For Hermits*.) The Contacts part covers the Outlook tools for keeping track of names, addresses, phone numbers, e-mail addresses, and general information.

Part VI: Journal

Outlook enables you to create handy little notes to jog your memory. You can place these little yellow notes, just like the real paper ones, anywhere in Outlook, just as you would place one on your refrigerator or your coworker's forehead, as a reminder of something to do.

Part VII: Notes

You can use the Journals module in Outlook to keep track of everything you do in Outlook. For example, you can track every activity related to a person in your address book, such as every conversation you have over the phone or every e-mail message you exchange.

Part VIII: Files and Folders

This part tells you how to use the rather facile Outlook facilities for dealing with files, folders, and all the other stuff on your computer.

Conventions Used in This Book

To keep this book brief and to the point, I assume that you're comfortable with Windows and Microsoft Office. If you're new to those packages, I strongly recommend the appropriate ...*For Dummies* books about those programs.

Because I'm a confessed keyboard freak, I prefer to show you keyboard shortcuts wherever possible. When you see

Ctrl+Z

it means that you press the Ctrl key and the letter *Z* at the same time. When you see

File⇨Open

it means that you click your mouse on the word *File* on the menu bar and then choose the Open command. The underlined letters are *hot keys,* which enable you to keep your hands on the keyboard. You can use hot keys to open the File menu by holding down the Alt key and the letter *F* at the same time and then releasing both keys and choosing the Open command by pressing the letter *O.*

What the Pictures Mean

I've sprinkled icons throughout this book to make things so clear that you really don't need me to explain them. That won't stop me from explaining them anyway, of course:

Information that can save you time or effort.

Alerts you to a problem to avoid.

Shows you the quickest way to do something.

Points out a feature of the program that seems nonsensical — because it *is* nonsensical.

Points you to a more complete explanation in the full-size, luxury edition of *Microsoft Outlook 2000 For Windows For Dummies.*

Points to a feature that requires you to be networked through Microsoft Exchange Server in order to take advantage of it.

Windows Here and There

Three main versions of Windows are now in use: Windows 95, Windows 98, and Windows NT 4. Because Outlook 2000 works with all these versions, just the word *Windows* is used in the text in this book. If something applies to just one of those versions, I tell you specifically.

Other Stuff

Microsoft Outlook gives you the tools you need for real desktop productivity: Whenever necessary, you can easily use each module without leaving your other Office applications. Microsoft plans even more features in the future. At least you know that there's more to Outlook than meets the eye. This book helps you discover more of it.

Part 1

All about Outlook

Outlook offers you much more than would fit in this itty-bitty volume. I stick to the important stuff so that you can leap right in and start making Outlook a valuable tool in your daily work.

The Outlook functions that are immediately useful are the Personal Information Management features. They show up as soon as you start the program. Microsoft cleverly designed Outlook to enable you to program and customize it to do almost anything you want that involves managing data. Some of the tasks that Outlook plans to do for you, such as store voice mail messages and advanced fax services, are still a gleam in some programmer's eye. In the meantime, I focus on what Outlook offers here and now.

In this part . . .

- About the screen
- Drag-and-drop
- Microsoft Exchange Server
- Microsoft Office and Outlook
- Options
- Specialized applications
- Outlook Express and other Outlook flavors
- Outlook today

About the Screen

After you start Outlook, you see a screen within a screen. The area along the top edge and left side of the screen offers a collection of menus and icons. These items enable you to control what you see and what you make happen on the other areas of the screen. The different parts of the Outlook screen have names:

Along the left side of the Outlook screen is the *Outlook bar*. It has large, clearly marked icons for each of the Outlook modules: Outlook Today, Inbox, Calendar, Contacts, Tasks, Journal, Notes, and Deleted Items. You can click any icon at any time to switch to a different module and then switch back, just like changing channels on your TV.

The Outlook bar also has three gray separator bars, named Outlook Shortcuts, My Shortcuts, and Other Shortcuts. You can click these separator bars to switch to a different section of the Outlook bar that has a different set of icons. You can add icons to any section of the Outlook bar. You can also add sections to the bar itself by right-clicking the Outlook bar. This action opens the shortcut menu, which enables you to choose the appropriate command.

The folder banner

The *folder banner* is the name of the area that sits below the toolbars and above the main part of the Outlook screen (known as the information viewer). The name of the folder or module you're using is displayed in large letters at the left end of the folder banner. The right end of the banner displays a large icon that is also used by the Outlook bar to represent the module you're using.

Other information also turns up from time to time on the folder banner, such as

✦ The alphabetical section of the Contact list you're viewing

✦ Whether you're using *filtering,* which enables you to limit the information displayed on the screen to items that meet certain criteria

✦ The Group By box when you're using grouped views

In addition, clicking the small, downward-pointing triangle next to the name of the module or folder on the left end of the folder banner reveals a copy of the folder list.

The folder list

The *folder list* gives you a quick peek behind the scenes at what's going on in Outlook. I leave the folder list closed most of the time. If you're interested, however, here's what goes on behind the scenes.

Outlook organizes into folders all the information you enter. Each Outlook module has its own folder. Although you usually change modules by clicking the icon for that module on the Outlook bar, you can also switch to a different module by clicking the folder for that module on the folder list. Every Outlook module that has an icon on the Outlook bar has a folder on the folder list, but not every folder on the folder list is represented by an icon on the Outlook bar. Because you can have more folders on the folder list than icons on the Outlook bar, you may have to use the folder list to go to a specific folder rather than click its icon on the Outlook bar.

To open the folder list, choose View➪Folder List from the menu bar. The folder list takes up so much space on the screen that I can't do much work. That's why I leave it closed most of the time.

The information viewer

The biggest part of the Outlook screen, on the lower-right side, is the *information viewer.* Whatever you ask Outlook to show you shows up in the information viewer. Dates in your Calendar, messages in your Inbox, and names on your Contact list all appear in the information viewer.

You can drag items from the information viewer to icons on the Outlook bar to create new types of Outlook items from the information you already have (*see also* "Drag-and-Drop," later in this part).

Menus

Like all Windows programs, Outlook has a *menu bar* across the top of the screen. To make a menu of commands appear, click your mouse on a menu name, such as File, Edit, or View. The underlined letter in a menu name is a *hot key;* holding down the Alt key while pressing that letter does the same thing as clicking the mouse on the menu name.

Menus in Outlook 2000 are divided into two parts. The most commonly used choices on a menu are shown when you click a menu. You may notice a double-arrow symbol at the bottom of the menu. Click the symbol to see more choices on the menu.

On-screen forms

Every time you either open an item or create a new item in Outlook, a *form* appears. This form either accepts the information you want to enter or contains the information you're viewing — or both. Each module has its own form, and each form has its own menus and toolbars.

You can also create your own forms with Outlook, or you can download new collections of forms from the Internet. For more information about customizing Outlook forms, get a copy of *Microsoft Outlook 2000 For Windows For Dummies,* by yours truly (IDG Books Worldwide, Inc.).

Status bar

The gray bar across the bottom of the Outlook screen is the *status bar,* which tells you how many items are displayed and a few other pieces of essential information.

Toolbars

Toolbars offer a quicker way to control Outlook than clicking menus. The Outlook *toolbar* changes as you switch between different modules or views, to offer you the most useful set of tools for the task you're doing at the moment. If you see a tool button and want to know what it does, let your mouse pointer hover over the button but don't click; a ToolTip box appears, revealing the name of the tool. Outlook 2000 has two toolbars you can choose from on the main screen: the Standard toolbar and the Advanced toolbar. The Advanced toolbar offers a larger selection of tools. You can pick the toolbar you want to use by choosing View➪Toolbars and clicking the name of the toolbar you want to see.

Drag-and-Drop

You can do a surprising amount of work without ever touching the keyboard. That little ol' mouse of yours can *drag* items from one part of Outlook and *drop* them on the icons on the Outlook bar to create new items. After you drop an item from one Outlook module into another, Outlook transforms the information and makes the item useful in a whole new way: An e-mail message can become a Contact item, for example, or a Contact item can become a Journal entry. This section shows some typical examples. You can find, naturally, more details in the other parts of this book.

Contact records created from e-mail messages

If someone sends you an e-mail message, you have all the information you need to create a new Contact record and enter that person on your Contact list.

To create a new Contact record, follow these steps:

1. Click the Inbox icon to see your current incoming messages.

2. Click the message icon in the first column of the list of messages for the message from a person whose name you want to add to your Contact list. Then drag the message to the Contacts icon to open a New Contact form.

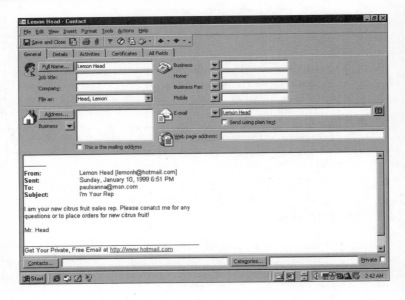

3. Enter in the appropriate text boxes whatever information you want to enter other than the e-mail address, which is already there. (*See also* Part V for more information.)

4. Click the Save and Close button (or press Alt+S).

A new contact is now part of your Contact list. Although you can drag any type of item to the Contacts icon, e-mail messages are the only items that make sense to drag there. Doing so saves you time by providing information you need in a Contact record anyway.

E-mail messages created from appointments

You can send an e-mail message informing someone of an existing appointment or inviting someone to attend a meeting. The person to whom you're sending the message gets an e-mail message, with the particulars of the appointment serving as the body of the message.

To send an e-mail message with information about an appointment, follow these steps:

1. Click the Calendar icon to open your list of appointments.

2. Drag an appointment to the Inbox icon to open a New Message form with details of the appointment filled in.

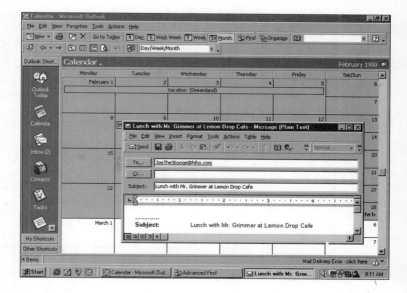

3. Fill in the e-mail address of the person to whom you want to send notice of the appointment, as well as any other information you want to include (*see* Part III for more about appointments).

4. Click Send (or press Alt+S).

If you and anyone you're inviting to the meeting are using a computer connected to a network that uses Microsoft Exchange Server, you can click the Meeting Planner tab on the Appointment form to check their schedules before calling the meeting. If you're not using Exchange Server, e-mail is your best bet for inviting others to attend your meeting or appointment.

E-mail messages created from your Contact list

If you've already entered a person's e-mail address on your Contact list, you have all you need to create an e-mail message for that person.

1. Click the Contacts icon to open the Contact list.

2. Drag to the Inbox icon the name of the person to whom you're sending a message. A New Message form opens with the contact's address already filled in.

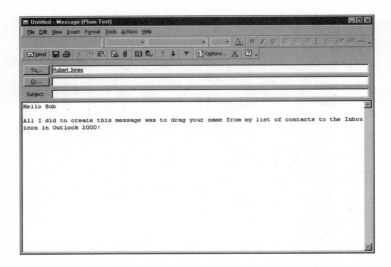

3. Enter whatever other information you want in the appropriate text boxes (*see* Part II for more information about e-mail).

4. Click Send (or press Alt+S).

If you're on an office network using Exchange Server, clicking Send sends your message directly to the recipient.

Journal entries created from a Contact record

You can create a Journal entry from any name on your Contact list. Use drag-and-drop to create a Journal entry with a link to the contact. Drag-and-drop goes beyond saving you the effort of entering contact information on the New Journal Entry form. You can hop right to the Contact record from the Journal entry to find the contact's address, phone number, or other information.

To create a Journal entry from a Contact record, follow these steps:

1. Click the Contacts icon to open the Contact list.

2. Drag the name of the contact from the Contact list to the Journal icon on the Outlook bar to open a New Journal Entry form.

3. Choose the type of Journal entry from the Entry Type list box. You can make a Journal entry for a letter, conversation, phone call, e-mail message, or any of the 20-odd choices available in the Entry Type list box. I like to make Journal entries of incoming phone calls.

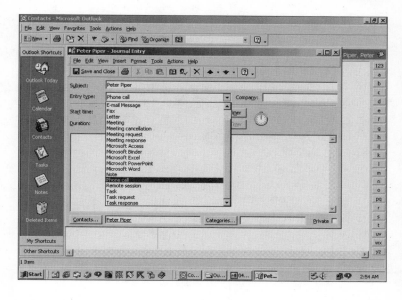

4. Fill in any other information in the appropriate text box.

5. Click the Save and Close button (or press Alt+S).

Your new entry is recorded in the Journal.

You can set up Outlook to make automatic Journal entries for new documents, e-mail messages, and AutoDialed phone calls. This automatic entry means that you don't need to create additional Journal entries for those events (*see* Part VI for more information about the Journal).

Text exchange with other Windows programs

I like to save snippets from various documents and Web pages in my collection of notes for later reference. The process of dragging text from other applications is easier to do than to explain, so bear with me.

To save text from other applications, follow these steps:

1. Select the information you want to save by dragging your mouse over the text you want to save. The text is highlighted to show what you've selected.

2. Hold down the Ctrl key while dragging the information from the original program to the Outlook icon on the Windows taskbar at the bottom of the screen. (The Outlook icon is labeled Inbox, Notes, or the name of whatever Outlook module you're using at the time.)

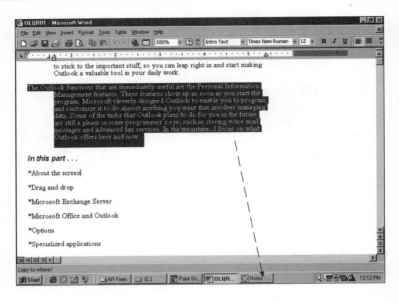

3. Hold the mouse on the Outlook icon without releasing the mouse button for a second or so while Outlook appears.

4. After Outlook appears, drag the mouse pointer over to the Notes icon (or any icon on the Outlook bar) and release the mouse button to see the note on your screen.

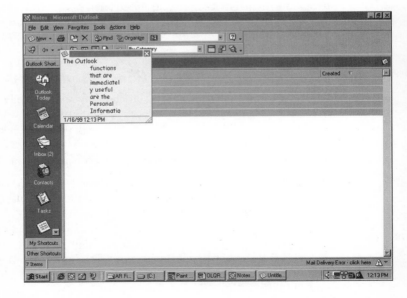

5. When your text appears in a note, press Esc to close the note.

Although you can drag text to any Outlook module, Notes is the most useful module to drag things to. In other modules, the text always ends up in the box at the bottom of the New Item form. You can always select and drag text up from the box at the bottom of the form after you've captured the information on the form.

Undeleting deleted items

You can delete any Outlook item by dragging the item to the Deleted Items icon on the Outlook bar. I don't go into detail about how to drag items to the Deleted Items folder.

Clicking the item you want to delete and then clicking the Delete button on the toolbar or pressing the Delete key on your keyboard is much easier.

You can easily use Undelete to bring items back, by dragging them from the Deleted Items folder.

To undelete deleted items, follow these steps:

1. Click the Deleted Items icon on the Outlook bar to open the list of deleted items.

2. Drag the deleted item you want to restore back to the icon of the module from which the item came (contacts to the Contacts icon and tasks to the Tasks icon, for example).

After you drag an item from the Deleted Items folder back to the folder from which it came, the item takes its place among all the other items in the folder, as though it had never been deleted.

Microsoft Exchange Server

If you use Outlook in an office connected to a network, you may have certain features that stand-alone (non-networked) Outlook users don't enjoy. The most important network features are available only if the network you're connected to uses *Microsoft Exchange Server*. It adds features, such as shared folders and custom applications for special needs. I don't explain Exchange Server in depth in this book. The following sections, however, show how you can use important features you may encounter if you're using both Outlook and Microsoft Exchange Server.

Public Folders

A Public Folder, in its simplest form, consists of a folder full of Outlook items that a large number of people can read and add to as they want. With the Public Folder, you can conduct conversations with a group of people more easily than by sending an e-mail message to everybody in a large group.

Follow these steps to take advantage of Public Folders if they are available to you:

1. Click the Folder List button on the toolbar to open the folder list.

2. Click the name of the folder you want to see. A list of the items in the folder appears in the information viewer.

3. To open the Discussion Item form, double-click the name of any item you want to read.

4. If you want to read the next item, click the Next Item button on the form toolbar or press Ctrl+>. The next item in the folder appears.

5. If you want to reply to an item you read, click the Reply icon on the Outlook bar; then enter your response and click Post to add your message to the other messages in the folder.

You can create Public Folders for any reason you want. You may have a Public Folder dedicated to conducting business discussions, making personal announcements, offering classified ads, or whatever.

One of the most confusing aspects of Outlook is that Microsoft assumes that everyone using Outlook is also using Microsoft Exchange Server. Many Outlook menus have commands you can't use without Exchange Server. You have to dig pretty deeply into the Outlook Help files to figure out which features require Exchange Server and which ones don't. Although some features work whether or not you have Exchange Server, they behave differently in different situations. Microsoft obviously wants everyone to use Outlook *and* Microsoft Exchange Server. In this book, I assume that you're *not* using Exchange Server; when Exchange Server is specifically required, I tell you.

Some other features of Microsoft Exchange Server

If you're one of the fortunate few using Outlook on a network with Microsoft Exchange Server, you can do some useful things with Outlook that non-networked users can't do:

✦ **Read Internet newsgroups:** If your network administrator
sees fit, you can read Internet newsgroups through Outlook
and Exchange Server. Internet *newsgroups* are places where
people all over the world can post messages about various
subjects and others can respond to those messages with
messages of their own. Newsgroups are much like the Public
Folders I describe in the preceding section in that they are a
public place where users can post information. Each Internet
newsgroup is organized to serve people who are interested in
a specific topic. Tens of thousands of newsgroups exist,
devoted to discussions about topics as varied as cooking,
dogs, movie stars, and, of course, nearly every type of
computer software.

✦ **Share your calendar with others:** Scheduling a meeting with
others in your organization is easier when you know who's
available and when. With Microsoft Exchange Server, you can
look at the calendar of each individual and find a time when
all of you are free and then schedule the meeting accordingly.
Outlook 2000 has a *Net Folders* feature that also enables you to
share calendar information with any other Outlook 2000 user
via e-mail. If you use Net Folders, you don't absolutely need
Exchange in order to share calendars, although Exchange
does the job more efficiently.

✦ **Synchronize offline folders:** Both Microsoft Exchange Server
and Outlook organize information into folders: Outlook stores
the folders on your computer, and Exchange stores folders on
a different computer — known as a *server* — which is located
someplace else on your office network. Exchange folders are
meant to be shared with other people, whereas usually only
one person uses a set of Outlook folders. If you use Outlook
on a laptop and you need to use information from Exchange
Server while you're traveling, you can create your own copy
of the Exchange folder on your laptop. When you return from
your trip with all your work finished, you can synchronize the
copy of the folder on your laptop that you've used to make it
match the copy that everyone shares on the company's
server.

Although I could go on extolling the benefits you get from
Microsoft Exchange Server, most folks have no choice about
whether the program is available to them. At the time I wrote this
book, only a small proportion of computer users also used
Microsoft Exchange Server; the computer business changes
quickly, however, so you have to wait and see.

Microsoft Office and Outlook

Outlook was originally introduced as part of the Microsoft Office suite. And, as you can guess, Outlook was designed to cooperate fully with other Office programs. Drag-and-drop techniques, cut and paste, and all sorts of other common tasks work throughout the suite. A few of the highlights are described in this section.

Introducing Office Assistant

The little critter that pops up every time you press the F1 key is the *Office Assistant.* You can leave the Assistant on-screen all the time if you want, or you can click the Close button in the upper-right corner of the Assistant window to make the Assistant go away.

When you ask for help, the Assistant opens a window in which you can type your question in plain English. In most cases, the Assistant makes sense of your question and then gives you a range of possible answers.

Office Assistant

If you leave the Office Assistant open all the time, it takes over most of the dialog boxes you usually see when you use Office applications. The result is that when you close an Outlook item, it's the Assistant that asks, "Do you want to save changes?"

Sometimes a small lightbulb appears in the upper-right corner of the Assistant's window. This lightbulb means that the Assistant has a tip in mind to help you do what it thinks you're trying to do. Fortunately, the Assistant remains quiet unless you click the bulb to get the hint.

Making Outlook talk to Word

Because Outlook was made to work well with Microsoft Word, it's no surprise that you can use the two in tandem. Oddly, Microsoft left out a few details, so this section describes some things you need to do to get the most from the two programs when you use them together.

If you want to have the power of Word at your disposal when you're creating e-mail, you have to tell Outlook that you want to use Word as your e-mail editor.

To use Word as your e-mail editor, follow these steps:

1. Choose Tools⇨Options from the Outlook menu to open the Options dialog box.

2. Click the Mail Format tab in the Options dialog box, and then choose Microsoft Word from the Send in This Message Format list box.

3. Click OK to close the Options dialog box.

After you choose Word as your e-mail editor, you can use the powerful formatting features of Word for all your e-mail messages. Elements such as bulleted lists, paragraph numbering, tables, graphics, and special text effects are available to you. These features wouldn't be available otherwise.

Remember that when you're using Word as your e-mail editor, many advanced formatting features you can add to your e-mail can be read only by recipients who also use Microsoft Word and Outlook. In some cases, using Word as your e-mail editor also makes Outlook perform somewhat slowly, so you may do just as well choosing plain text or HTML as your message format.

You can insert an address from your Outlook Contact list into a Word document by clicking a single button. Unfortunately, Microsoft didn't put that button on the Word toolbar, so you have to add it.

To add the Address Book button to the Word toolbar, follow these steps:

1. Open Microsoft Word and then choose Tools⇨Customize to open the Customize dialog box.

2. Click the Commands tab to view the list of available commands.

3. Click Insert in the Categories box to reveal the list of Insert commands on the Commands list on the right side of the screen.

4. Scroll down to the words *Address Book* near the end of the Commands list box.

5. Drag the Address Book icon up to the Word toolbar. The Address Book icon joins the other icons on the toolbar.

Whew! Fortunately, you have to install the Address Book icon only once. After you install the Address Book, you can go right ahead and insert an address from your Outlook Contact list anywhere in any Word document in a jiffy.

To insert an address from your Outlook Contact list, follow these steps:

1. Open any document in Microsoft Word.

2. Click your mouse at the point in the document where you want to place an address. The insertion point (a vertical flashing bar) appears at the spot where you click.

3. Click the Address Book button on the Word toolbar to open the Select Name dialog box.

4. After the Select Names dialog box opens, choose Contacts from the drop-down list to make the names from your Contact list appear.

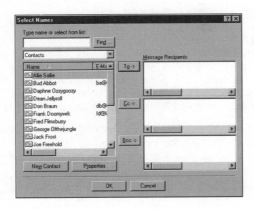

5. From the list at the bottom of the Select Name dialog box, choose the name of the person whose address you want to enter.

6. Click OK to make the address of the person you picked appear in your document.

As you use the Address Book icon, you may notice the scroll-down button (triangle) just to the right of the icon. After you click the triangle, a list appears that contains the last 16 people whose addresses you entered by using the Address Book icon. To enter the address of one of the 16 people listed, just click his or her name; you don't have to go through the Select Name dialog box.

Making Outlook work with PowerPoint

If you're making a PowerPoint presentation at a meeting, you may need to make a note to do something as a result of the meeting. You can use the PowerPoint Meeting Minder feature to enter items on your Outlook task list without leaving your PowerPoint presentation.

To enter items by using the PowerPoint Meeting Minder feature, follow these steps:

1. In PowerPoint, choose Tools⇨Meeting Minder to open the Meeting Minder dialog box.

2. Click the Action Items tab.

3. Fill in the appropriate information in the Description, Assigned To, and Due Date boxes.

4. Click Add to make each item appear on the list of Action Items.

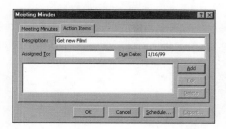

5. After your list is complete, click the Export button to open the Meeting Minder Export dialog box.

6. Click the check box that says Post Action Items to Microsoft Outlook.

7. Click Export Now to export action items to your task list. The dialog boxes disappear, and you return to your PowerPoint presentation. Later, when you check your task list, you see listed there the action items you exported.

Options

You can customize Outlook to meet your needs. Adding, renaming, or deleting parts of the screen are easy to do, according to how you work. You can also make Outlook begin each session by showing you the information that you think is most important.

Add an icon to the Outlook bar

After you get used to using Outlook, you may want to create more icons on the Outlook bar. Because each icon on the Outlook bar is a shortcut to a folder or resource on your computer, you can save some time by adding a few well-chosen icons.

The principle for adding icons is the same no matter what you're creating an icon to do.

Follow these steps to add an icon to the Outlook bar:

1. Choose View⇨Folder List.

2. Right-click a folder for which you want to add an icon to the Outlook bar. The shortcut menu appears.

3. Choose Add to Outlook Bar from the shortcut menu.

AutoArchive

You can save a great deal of information in Outlook. After you store enough items, however, Outlook starts to slow down. To keep the program speedy, Outlook periodically sends older items to the archive file. Although the files are still available, Outlook doesn't have to dredge them up every time you start the program.

You can set up Outlook to send items to the archives automatically after the items reach a certain age.

To set up automatic archiving, follow these steps:

1. Choose Tools⇨Options to open the Options dialog box.

2. Click the Other tab.

3. Click the AutoArchive button to open the AutoArchive dialog box.

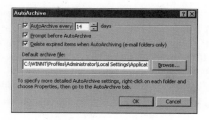

4. Click the check box that says AutoArchive Every XX Days and fill in the number of days you want between automatic archive sessions. If the box is already checked and you want the AutoArchiving feature on, leave the box alone.

5. Click OK to close the AutoArchive dialog box.

6. Click OK again to close the Options dialog box.

After AutoArchiving is set up, whenever Outlook is ready to send items to the archive, you see a dialog box that asks whether you want the items sent to the archive.

If you choose not to use AutoArchiving, you can always archive items manually by choosing File⇨Archive.

Data files

All the items you create with Outlook and all the e-mail you send and receive are stored in one enormous file, called a *message store*. The filename of your message store ends with the letters PST. If you're trying to find your Outlook files so that you can back them up, use the Windows Find utility and search for files named *.PST. The largest file you find by that name is probably your Outlook data file.

Copying your MAILBOX.PST file to a floppy disk is not really an option. The file is usually 10 or 20 times too large to fit on a floppy disk.

Undo

Undo can be a lifesaver when you goof and need to fix your goof quickly: Just press Ctrl+Z. Outlook has only a one-level undo, which means that if you make two goofs in a row, you can only undo the last one. If you goof and then change modules by clicking an icon on the Outlook bar, you can't go back and undo the mistake.

Specialized Applications

Outlook was designed with expansion in mind. Names, addresses, and files are important things to keep track of. Clever programmers release new modules for Outlook every day. The Microsoft Web site on the Internet offers a collection of sample applications to expand the range of things you can do with Outlook. You can go to the Microsoft Web site directly from Outlook.

You can get these sample applications free from the Microsoft Web site on the Internet. The sample applications include expense report applications, project management programs, and even cute little programs for keeping your recipes or making entries in your diary.

To pick up (or *download,* in tech talk) your free sample applications, follow these steps:

1. Choose Help⇨Office on the Web⇨Free Stuff to log on to the Microsoft site on the World Wide Web and see the list of free sample applications available for Outlook.

2. Click the name of a sample application you want to use, such as Expense Reports, Project Management, Recipes, or Diary. If your browser is Microsoft Internet Explorer, a dialog box appears, asking whether you want to run the file or save it to disk.

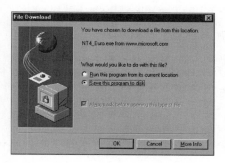

3. Choose Save This Program to Disk.

The Save dialog box opens, showing you the name of the folder in which your file will be saved.

Note the name of the folder in the Save In box; that's where you install the new sample application after downloading the file. If you're not sure about which folder is the best place to save the file you're about to download, click the scroll-down menu (triangle) in the Save In box; then choose Desktop to make your new file go to the Windows desktop.

4. Click OK and wait for the File Transfer dialog box that shows up to disappear.

After a few minutes, the File Transfer dialog box disappears, which means that the file you need in order to install your new sample application is on your computer. Now you're ready to install the sample application to make it work in Outlook.

A word of caution: Many of the sample applications you find on the Microsoft Web site are useful only if you're using Outlook on a network that is also running Microsoft Exchange Server. Microsoft sometimes doesn't tell you which applications are useful for stand-alone (non-network) users, so, unfortunately, you're on your own. If you're on a network with Exchange Server, check with your network administrator before adding new applications.

After you download your brand-new sample application, you have to install it. Double-click the icon for the new file and follow the instructions that appear in the dialog boxes.

Because each sample application is a little different, you have to read the instructions carefully. I wish that I could give you full instructions for all the sample applications, but because Microsoft offers new sample applications every week, I can't predict what you'll be dealing with.

Some Outlook applications are *version-specific,* which means that they work with only a specific version of the product. For example, an application built for Outlook 97 may not work with Outlook 2000. Be sure to read any information supplied about the application to ensure that it works with your version of Outlook.

Outlook Express and Other Outlook Flavors

The folks at Microsoft were mighty proud after they released Outlook — so proud, in fact, that they gave the name Outlook to a second, totally different product a few weeks later. *Outlook Express* is a program that used to be called Internet Mail and News before going big-time and getting a new name. Although I'm sure that Microsofties find the new names perfectly sensible, I become very confused when I have to deal with two different products that go by the same name.

Like regular Outlook, Outlook Express can exchange e-mail. But Outlook Express can't do many of the fancy tricks with your mail that you can do with regular Outlook. For example, you can't drag an e-mail message to the Contacts folder to create a new Contact record or flag messages to remind you to take action.

Outlook Express can do tricks that regular Outlook hasn't learned yet, however, such as read Internet newsgroups. (*Newsgroups* are places on the Internet where people can read each other's messages and post replies to any message.) *See also* the discussion about Public Folders, in the section "Microsoft Exchange Server," earlier in this part. The Public Folders are similar to newsgroups, except that newsgroups are available to anyone on the Internet. Public Folders can be used only by people you work with.

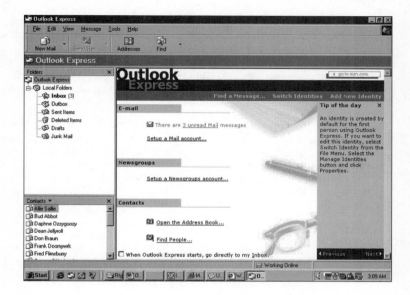

If you have Outlook 2000, you also have Outlook Express. You can start Outlook Express by choosing View⇨Go To⇨News from the Outlook menu bar. After you start Outlook Express from within Outlook, you see a special version of Outlook Express that only enables you to read and contribute to Internet newsgroups.

Microsoft has hinted strongly that someday regular Outlook (which you have to pay for) will be able to read Internet newsgroups, just as you can with Outlook Express (which is free). Don't worry if this situation confuses you: It confuses everybody. For more information about Outlook Express, see my full-size version of this book, *Microsoft Outlook 2000 For Windows For Dummies,* published by IDG Books Worldwide, Inc.

Outlook Today

Outlook is designed to pull all your personal information into one handy package. The Outlook Today page pulls to a single screen all the Outlook data you're likely to need to see at any moment. All you have to do is click the Outlook Today icon on the Outlook bar. If you can't see the icon, choose Go⇨Outlook Today from the menu bar.

The Outlook Today page is similar to a page on the World Wide Web. Most of the text on the page is composed of *hypertext,* which means that if you click the text, the screen changes to show you the full text of the Outlook module or item it refers to. For example, if you click the word *Mail* on the Outlook Today page, the screen switches to a view of your Inbox and displays all the messages that are waiting for you.

I like to print Outlook Today to help remind me of what I need to do each day. That's the best way I know of to see a single summary of my most current appointments, tasks, and messages. If you want to print your Outlook Today page, click the Outlook Today icon on the Outlook bar and then choose File⇨Print from the menu bar.

Part 11

E-Mail

The e-mail Inbox is the first thing you see when you start Outlook, and if e-mail is the only thing you ever use Outlook for, you still get your money's worth.

You can exchange e-mail with television personalities, the White House, and yes, even Microsoft (although you may have trouble getting someone there to answer).

When you use Outlook to create and receive your e-mail, you have lots of options for viewing, sorting, and organizing your messages that can make your messages more useful. You can assign a category to each message and then group by category the messages you've sent to review what you've done.

In this part . . .

✔ **Introducing the Inbox screen**

✔ **Creating, sending, and printing e-mail messages**

✔ **Answering your e-mail**

✔ **Sending and receiving e-mail online**

✔ **Using views**

About the Inbox Screen

The main Inbox screen enables you to look at a list of your e-mail and helps you manage the messages you send and receive. You can create folders for storing each message according to what the message is about, who sent it to you, or when you received it.

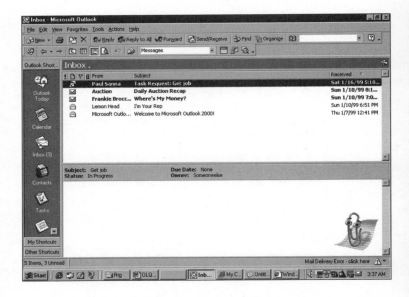

You can change the arrangement of what you see in the Inbox by changing the view. (A *view* is a method of organizing the information you see in Outlook.) Each view has a name, such as Message, AutoPreview, or By Conversation Topic.

To change from one view to another, simply choose View➪Current View and pick the view you want from the list that appears.

Accessing your Inbox

Your Inbox contains your list of incoming e-mail. Even if you've never exchanged e-mail with anybody or even if you don't *know* anybody, you see at least one message in your Inbox the first time you start Outlook — the "Welcome to Microsoft Outlook" message. Isn't that nice of Microsoft?

To open and read an e-mail message, follow these steps:

1. Switch to the Inbox by clicking the Inbox icon on the Outlook bar.

2. Double-click the title of the message you want to read. The message opens, using the entire screen so that you can read your message.

3. Press Esc to close the message screen.

If you want to read the message that follows on your list, press Ctrl+>.

Opening the Message form

Messages in Outlook are displayed on a *form*. A form contains various fields, and these fields store the information about the message you're interested in, such as the text of the message, who sent it, when it was sent, its priority, and more. Whenever you want to read or write a message, open the Message form by double-clicking the title of the message in the Inbox (or whatever folder you filed the message in). Whenever you double-click the title of a message, the Message form screen appears. The Message form has many of the same tools and menus as the main Outlook screen but also includes at the bottom a large message box that contains either the message you're reading or space for the message you're about to write.

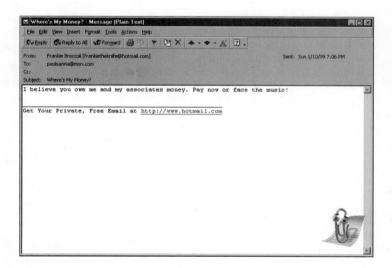

The little figures on the Message form toolbar do things that are specific to writing and reading e-mail messages, such as reply, print, or mark as high or low priority; the up and down arrows enable you to read the next message on your Inbox list.

Creating and Sending Messages

If you know an e-mail address, you can send a message. You don't even need to have anything to say, although it's usually a good idea to have a thought or two worth sending so that people find your e-mail worth reading.

To create a message, follow these steps:

1. Switch to the Inbox by clicking the Inbox icon on the Outlook bar to show your list of messages.

2. Click the New Mail Message button (or press Ctrl+N) to open the New Message form.

3. Click the To text box and enter the e-mail address of the person to whom you're sending the message.

For people whose e-mail addresses you've included on your Contact list, just enter the person's name. If Outlook knows the e-mail address of the person whose name you enter, a solid black underline appears under the name.

Another approach is to click the To button to open the Select Name dialog box. Then double-click the name of the person to whom you're sending the message from the list on the left side of the box; click OK to return to your Message form.

4. Click the Cc text box and enter the e-mail address of the people to whom you want to send a copy of your message.

5. Enter the subject of the message in the Subject box.

6. Enter the text of your message in the text box.

7. Click the Send button (or press Alt+S) to close the Message form and send your message on its way.

If you send your e-mail over an online service, you also have to press F5 to deliver your message from the Outbox to your online service. If you're on an office network that uses Microsoft Exchange Server, your message goes directly to the recipient when you click Send.

Attaching files to your messages

Whenever you want to send someone a document, a picture, or a spreadsheet that you don't want to include in the message itself, you can add it to the message as an *attachment*. You don't even have to send an actual message; just save the file you're working on and send it along as an attachment.

Follow these steps to send an attachment:

1. Switch to the Inbox by clicking the Inbox icon on the Outlook bar.

2. Choose File⇨New⇨Mail Message (or press Ctrl+Shift+M) to open the New Message form.

3. Click the paper-clip button on the Message form toolbar. The list of files appears.

4. Click the name of the file you want to send. The filename is highlighted to show that you've selected it.

5. Click Insert. The list of files disappears, and an icon representing your file appears in the text box on the Message form.

6. Enter your message if you have a message to send. You don't have to send a message if you don't have anything to say.

7. Click the To button to open the Select Name dialog box.

8. Select a name from your address book.

9. Click the To button to move the name you selected to the Message Recipients box on the right side of the dialog box.

10. Click OK to close the Select Name dialog box and return to the Message form.

11. Click the Subject text box and enter a subject for your message.

12. Click the Send button to close the Message form.

If you want to send a document by e-mail while you're creating the document in a Microsoft Office application, you can eliminate most of this procedure by choosing File➪Send To➪Mail Recipient and then following Steps 7 through 12.

Formatting message text

You can spice up your messages with text formatting — such as boldface, italics, or different typefaces — whether you use Outlook alone or with Microsoft Office. You can also tell Outlook to use Microsoft Word 2000 as your e-mail editor, which means that every time you open an e-mail message, Microsoft Word steps in and automatically adjusts the appearance of the message. Whenever you create a new message with Word as your e-mail editor, you have the power to add fancy-looking elements to your message, such as tables and special text effects (like flashing text), and you can use all the other powerful features of Word.

The shortcoming to using Word as your e-mail editor is that you have to wait several seconds for Word to launch and format each message before you read it. If you're too impatient to wait a few seconds for each message to be formatted (I'll admit it: I am), you can get away with not using Word as your e-mail editor.

To format text in a message without using Microsoft Word as your e-mail editor, use the buttons on the Formatting toolbar on the Message form.

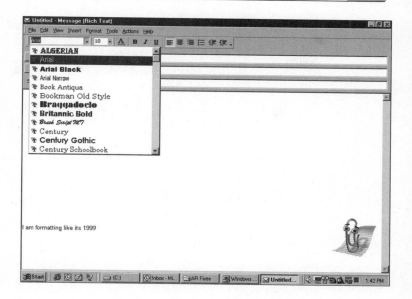

If you've ever used a word processor in Windows, the steps you follow to format text in an Outlook message should be familiar to you: Just click the button for the type of formatting you want to add to your text, and then type your text:

+ **To format text you've already typed:** Hold down the mouse button and drag the mouse over the text to select it. Then click the button for the type of formatting you want to add to your text, such as bold or italics.

+ **To set the typeface of your text:** Click the scroll-down button at the end of the font menu and choose the name of the font you want to use.

+ **To set the size of your text:** Click the scroll-down button on the font size menu and highlight the font size you want.

+ **To set the color of your text:** Click the color button and choose a color. You can choose from only a few colors, but because your choices include teal, fuchsia, and aqua, you can certainly find something to match any décor.

+ **To make your text bold, italic, or underlined:** Click the Bold, Italic, or Underline button (or press Ctrl+B, Ctrl+I, or Ctrl+U, respectively).

✦ **To align your text to the left, center, or right:** Click the Align Left, Center, or Align Right button. (I'd bet that you're starting to see a pattern here.)

✦ **To create a bulleted list:** Click the Bullets button. (This is not the button to click when you want to shoot your computer.)

✦ **To indent your text:** Click the Increase Indent button. To reduce the amount of space you've indented your text, click the Decrease Indent button.

When you send e-mail to people who don't use Outlook, the formatting you apply in Outlook often gets lost. Although you may enjoy seeing all your messages when you type them in bold fuchsia, many of your readers won't get the same pleasure when they read your messages.

Indicating message importance

Some messages are very important to both you and the person receiving the message. Other messages aren't so important, but you send them as a matter of routine to keep people informed. Outlook enables you to designate the importance of a message to help your recipients make good use of their time. When you open the Message form to create a message, two icons on the Message form toolbar enable you to select the importance of your message:

 ✦ **To assign High importance:** Click the Importance: High button on the Message form toolbar.

 ✦ **To assign Low importance:** Click the Importance: Low button on the Message form toolbar.

An icon corresponding to the importance of the message appears in the first column of the Message List.

Marking messages as personal, private, or confidential

You can designate any message you create as either personal, private, or confidential. How you designate the message makes little difference to Outlook. Personal and confidential messages are no different from any other message.

Private messages differ slightly from other messages in that, when you reply to or forward a private message, other Outlook users can't change the text of the message you send.

Follow these steps to make your message personal, private, or confidential while you're creating the message:

1. Click the Options button on the message toolbar to view the Options dialog box.

2. Click the scroll-down button at the right end of the Sensitivity box to see the available choices.

3. Choose Normal, Personal, Private, or Confidential.

4. Choose File⇨Close (or press Alt+F4) to close the message screen.

Messages marked personal, private, or confidential (especially messages on a corporate LAN) can still be read by people other than your intended recipient.

Saving copies of your messages

Outlook normally saves all sent messages in your Sent Items folder, but you can turn off this option. If you've turned this feature off, follow these steps to turn it back on:

1. Choose Tools⇨Options to open the Options dialog box.

2. Click the E-Mail Options button.

3. Click the Save Copies of Messages in Sent Items Folder option so that a check mark appears in the check box.

4. Click OK to close the Options dialog box.

I find it extremely handy to have copies of my sent messages available. I use them for recordkeeping and checking my work and sometimes just to be sure that a message went out.

Spell checking

Heaven knows you want to spell everything correctly when you send out an e-mail message. Who knows how many people will see the message or whether someone on an archeological dig a million years from now will discover your old messages? Fortunately, you can spell-check all your messages before sending them out:

1. Choose Tools⇨Spelling (or press F7) to start the spelling checker. If everything is perfect, a dialog box opens, saying that the spelling check is complete. If so, you can click OK and get on with your life.

2. In the highly unlikely event that you've misspelled something, the Spelling dialog box opens and shows you the error (it's probably the computer's fault) along with a list of suggested (that is, correct) spellings.

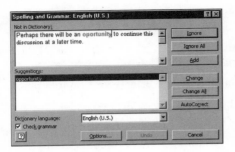

3. If one of the suggested spellings is the one you really meant, click the spelling you want. If none of the suggested spellings is quite what you have in mind, enter the spelling you want in the Change To box.

4. Click the Change button.

5. If any other errors are found, repeat Steps 3 and 4 until you've eradicated all misspellings.

Although the spelling checker often thinks that technical terms, like WYSIWYG, and proper names, like Englebert Humperdinck, are misspellings (well, maybe they are), you can increase your spelling checker's vocabulary by clicking the Add button when the spelling checker zeroes in on words like those. You can also click Ignore if the spelling checker stops on a weird word you encounter infrequently.

If you've chosen to use Microsoft Word as your e-mail editor (*see also* "Making Outlook talk to Word" in Part I), a wavy red underline appears beneath misspelled words as soon as you type them. When you see a wavy red underline beneath a word, just correct the spelling right then and there so that you don't have to use the spelling checker. When you right-click a misspelled word, a shortcut menu appears with the correct spelling; click the correct spelling and you can go right on entering text.

Using stationery

Stationery is designed to make your messages convey a visual impression about you. You can make your message look uniquely important, businesslike, or just plain fun with the right choice of stationery:

1. Choose Actions⇨New Mail Message Using⇨More Stationery. The Select a Stationery dialog box appears, with a list of each type of stationery you can choose.

2. Double-click the type of stationery you want to use.

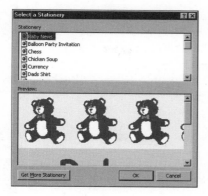

3. Fill in your message.

4. Click the To button to open the Select Name dialog box.

5. Double-click the name of the person to whom you want to send the message. This action copies the name to the Message Recipients list.

6. Click OK to close the Select Name dialog box.

7. Click Send to close the Message form and send your message along.

If the New Mail Message Using command on the Actions menu isn't black and doesn't work when you click it, you have to turn the feature on. Choose Tools⇨Options, click the Mail Format tab, and then choose HTML from the scroll-down menu at the top of the Mail Format page.

Handling Incoming Messages

You can reply to messages while you read them or you can wait until later.

Sending a reply

To reply to a message, follow these steps:

1. Switch to the Inbox by clicking the Inbox icon on the Outlook bar.

2. Double-click the title of the message to which you want to reply. Doing so shows the text of the message to which you're replying. You don't absolutely have to open a message to send a reply; you can click the name of a message once to select the message to reply to and then click the Reply button.

3. If you want to reply only to the people who are named on the From line, click the Reply button (or press Alt+R) to open the New Message form.

4. If you want to reply to the people who are named on the Cc line in addition to the people named on the From line, click the Reply to All button (or press Alt+L) to open the New Message form.

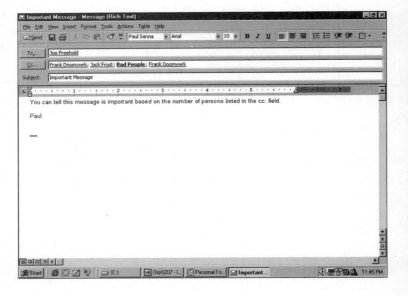

5. Enter your reply in the message box.

6. Click the Send button (or press Alt+S) to close the New Message form and send your message on its way.

The text of the message to which you're replying is automatically included in your reply unless you turn that option off by choosing Tools⇨Options and then selecting your options on the Reading tab.

Deleting a message

If you get mail from the Internet, you can expect lots of junk mail. You may also get lots of e-mail at work. I understand that Bill Gates gets scads of e-mail. Maybe that's why deleting messages in Outlook is so easy.

To delete a message, just follow these steps:

1. Switch to the Inbox by clicking the Inbox icon on the Outlook bar.

2. Click the title of the message you want to delete.

3. Click the Delete button on the toolbar or press the Delete key to make your message disappear.

If you accidentally delete something you meant to save, choose Edit⟹Undo Delete (or press Ctrl+Z) right away, and your message reappears.

Flagging your e-mail messages as a reminder

Some people use their incoming e-mail messages as an informal task list. Flagging is designed to make it easier to use your Inbox as a task list by adding individual reminders to each message you get (or even to messages you send).

Follow these steps to flag a message:

1. Switch to the Inbox by clicking the Inbox icon on the Outlook bar.

2. Double-click the message you want to flag, and the message reopens.

3. Choose Actions⟹Flag for Follow Up (or press Ctrl+Shift+G) to open the Flag for Follow Up dialog box.

4. Click the Flag To text box and enter your reminder, such as **Call headquarters**. You can also click the scroll-down button at the end of the Flag To text box and choose a reminder, such as Follow Up.

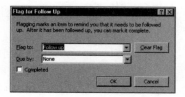

5. Click the Due By box and type the date on which you want the reminder flag to appear. Remember that you can enter dates in plain English by entering something like **Next Wednesday** or **In three weeks** and let Outlook figure out the actual date.

6. Click OK.

A little red flag appears next to your message in the Inbox. Another clever way you can take advantage of flagging is to attach a flag to a message when you're sending it to someone else. If you flag a message you're sending to someone else, a reminder pops up on her computer at the time you designate. I would bet that Bill Gates sends out lots of flagged messages, wouldn't you?

My, how time flies! If you've put a flag on a message that's due to appear before you're ready to do what the flag calls for, follow these steps to change the due date:

1. Switch to the Inbox by clicking the Inbox icon on the Outlook bar.

2. Double-click the message to open the Message form.

3. Choose Actions⇨Flag for Follow Up (or press Ctrl+Shift+G) to open the Flag for Follow Up dialog box.

4. Click the Reminder box and type the new date for when you want the reminder flag to appear.

5. Click OK to close the Flag for Follow Up dialog box.

6. Press Esc to close the Message form.

Your message is still flagged as it was before, but the reminder pops up at a different time or displays a different message.

Forwarding a message

If you get a message you want to pass on to someone else, just forward it:

1. Switch to the Inbox by clicking the Inbox icon on the Outlook bar.

2. Click the title of the message you want to forward. This action highlights the message.

3. Click the Forward button on the Outlook toolbar (or press Ctrl+F) to open the New Message form.

4. Click the To text box and enter the e-mail address of the person to whom you're forwarding the message.

5. Click the Cc text box and enter the e-mail addresses of the people to whom you want to forward a copy of your message.

6. In the text box, enter any comments you want to add to the message.

7. Click the Send button (or press Alt+S) to close the Message form and send your message on its way.

You can also forward a message as you read it by clicking the Forward button on the Message form toolbar, which is visible when you open a message to read it.

Marking messages as Read or Unread

Outlook notices which messages you've read and which messages you haven't read. AutoPreview shows you only the first few lines of messages you haven't read, and Unread Messages view hides messages after you've read them.

You may want to mark a message as Unread even though you've read it; for example, if you don't have time to deal with the message the first time you see it, you may want to be reminded to read it again. You also may mark a message as Read if you see all you need to know in the three-line AutoPreview.

Follow these steps to mark a message as Read if you haven't read it and don't plan to:

1. Switch to the Inbox by clicking the Inbox icon on the Outlook bar.

2. Click the title of the message you want to mark as Read. This step highlights the message.

3. Choose Edit➪Mark as Read (or press Ctrl+Q).

To mark a message as Unread, follow the same steps, but choose Edit➪Mark as Unread instead.

Previewing messages

Because you can usually get the gist of an incoming e-mail message from the first few lines, Outlook shows you the first few lines of all unread messages, if you want. Although the AutoPreview feature is turned on the first time you use Outlook, you can also turn it off.

To turn AutoPreview on, follow these steps:

1. Switch to the Inbox by clicking the Inbox icon on the Outlook bar.

2. Choose View➪AutoPreview.

AutoPreview shows you the first few lines of the messages you haven't read yet. You can mark messages as Read or Unread to keep the AutoPreview pane open as you want.

AutoPreview may be the only way you ever want to view your Inbox. If you get a large number of messages, previewing them saves time. You can also take advantage of the preview pane to look at the contents of each message in the lower half of the information viewer while your list of messages appears in the upper half. To turn the preview pane on (or off) choose View⇨Preview Pane.

Saving a message as a file

You may want to save the contents of a message you receive so that you can use the text in another program. For example, you may want to use a desktop publishing program to add the text to your monthly newsletter or even to your page on the Internet.

To save a message as a text file, follow these steps:

1. Choose File⇨Save As (or press F12) to open the Save As dialog box.

2. Click the scroll-down button at the end of the Save In box to choose the drive to which you want to save the file.

3. Double-click the name of the folder in which you want to save the file to reveal the list of files in the folder.

4. Click the File Name text box and type the name you want to give the file.

5. If you want to change the type of the file, click the scroll-down button at the end of the Save As Type box and then choose a file type.

6. Click Save (or press Enter) to close the Save As dialog box.

Your message is saved as a text file in the folder you clicked. You can open the text file with any word processing program.

Setting options for replies

You can use the Options dialog box to control the way messages look when you send replies. If you're not fussy about things like that, you can leave this option alone and let Outlook take care of the formatting for you.

If you want to change the options for your replies, follow these steps:

1. Choose Tools⇨Options to open the Options dialog box.

2. Click the E-Mail Options button to show the choices available for message replies and forwarded messages.

3. Click the triangle at the right end of the When Replying to a Message box to reveal the list of styles available to you for replies.

4. Choose the style you prefer to use for replies. As you choose different styles, the little diagram on the right side of the box changes to show what your choice looks like.

5. Click the scroll-down button at the right end of the When Forwarding a Message box. Another diagram to the right of the menu shows what your choice looks like.

6. Choose the style you prefer to use for forwarding messages.

7. Click OK to close the Options dialog box.

If you're using Microsoft Word as your e-mail editor, you can also take advantage of the powerful features for formatting text that come with Word, including tables, bullets and numbering, and Autoformatting. For more information about what you can do with Microsoft Word, see *Word 2000 For Windows For Dummies,* by Dan Gookin (IDG Books Worldwide, Inc.).

Tagging replies with your name

When you reply to an e-mail message, Outlook includes in your reply the text of the original message. Including the original text helps the person you're replying to remember what you're talking about. Whenever you mix what you've written with what the other person wrote in the first place, however, the message can get confusing. Outlook gives you the option of automatically inserting your name before everything you add to a reply.

Follow these steps to turn this option on (or off):

1. Choose Tools➪Options to open the Options dialog box.

2. Click the E-Mail Options button to show the choices available for message replies and forwarded messages.

3. Click the Mark My Comments With check box. A check mark appears in the box.

4. In the Mark My Comments With text box, enter the text you want to accompany your annotations.

5. Click OK.

Using the Rules Wizard

The Rules Wizard reads your incoming and outgoing e-mail and takes an action of your choice. You can make Outlook display a pop-up announcement when important messages arrive or make a rude noise when you get messages from certain people, or it can just file certain types of messages in certain folders.

Wizards are little tools Microsoft adds to all Office programs to guide you through multistep processes and help you make the choices you need to make. The Rules Wizard asks you questions at each step in the process of creating a rule to help you create the rule you want.

You can create literally thousands of different kinds of rules with the Rules Wizard. As you explore this feature, you discover many types of rules that you'll find useful. I describe only one rule here, which I think that most people find useful; this one moves to a certain folder a message that arrives from a certain person.

Follow these steps to create a rule:

1. If you're not in the Inbox, click the Inbox icon on the Outlook bar.

2. Choose <u>T</u>ools➪Ru<u>l</u>es Wizard to open the Rules Wizard dialog box.

3. Click the New button to open a dialog box for creating new rules.

4. Choose the type of rule you want to create by clicking the box cleverly named Which Type of Rule Do You Want to Create? The Rules Wizard offers several common types of rules you might want to create, such as Move New Messages from Someone, Assign Categories to Sent Messages, or Notify Me When Important Messages Arrive.

5. Click the first piece of underlined text in the Rule Description box, which is *people or distribution list*. Your address book opens to enable you to choose the name of a person to put into your rule.

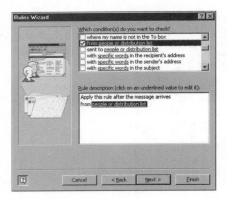

6. Choose the name of the person whose messages you want to move to a new folder; for example, if you want to move your boss's name from your address book. When you do, your boss's name replaces the words *people or distribution list*.

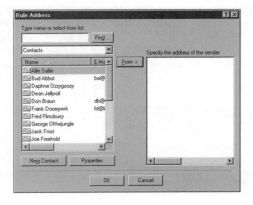

7. Click the next piece of underlined text in the Rule Description box — the word specified. Another dialog box opens to enable you to choose the folder to which you want to move the message.

8. Click the name of the folder to which you want to move messages. The name of the folder you choose appears in the sentence in the Rule Description box.

9. Click Finish to complete your rule. The first Rules Wizard dialog box appears with a list of all your rules. Each rule has a check box next to it. You can turn rules on and off by clicking the check boxes; if a check mark appears next to a rule, the rule is turned on; otherwise, the rule is turned off.

10. Click OK to close the Rules Wizard.

You don't have to limit yourself to making rules for incoming mail. You can also tell the Rules Wizard to act on the messages you send out, such as attaching flags or assigning categories to messages that go to the people you designate or to messages that have certain words on the subject line.

Managing Folders

Although you can leave all your incoming e-mail messages in your Inbox if you want, filing your messages in another folder makes more sense because you can see at a glance which messages you've already dealt with and classified and which ones have just arrived in your Inbox. I like to move messages out of my Inbox as soon as I've read them or taken appropriate action. For example, in the course of writing this book, I received dozens of messages about Outlook and the book. I saved all the messages about this book in a specific folder so that I don't have to waste time sorting through hundreds of old messages about other subjects when I need to find a message related to the book. I also like to keep the Inbox empty as often as possible; that way, I know that if I see something sitting in my Inbox, it's new.

Creating a folder

Before you can file messages in a new folder, you have to create the folder:

1. Click the Inbox icon to switch to your Inbox (if you're not already there).

2. Choose File⇨New⇨Folder (or press Ctrl+Shift+E) to open the Create New Folder dialog box.

3. Click the word *Inbox* on the list of folders at the bottom of the Create New Folder dialog box to highlight it.

4. In the Name text box, type a name for your new folder.

5. Click OK to close the Create New Folder dialog box.

Although you can create as many folders as you want, you can find things more easily if you minimize the number of folders you have to search.

Moving messages to another folder

After you've created extra folders for sorting and saving your incoming messages, you can move new messages to the different folders when they arrive.

To move messages to another folder, follow these steps:

1. Switch to the Inbox by clicking the Inbox icon on the Outlook bar.

2. Click the title of the message you want to move to highlight the message title.

3. Drag the message to the icon on the Outlook bar for the folder in which you want to store it. The name of the file disappears from the list in the Inbox.

The folder to which you want to move the message isn't always visible on the Outlook bar. If the folder to which you want to move your message isn't visible on the Outlook bar, choose Edit⇨Move to Folder to make a more complete list of folders appear (*see also* "The folder list," in Part I). Then you can click the folder in which you want to file your message and press Enter.

 After you've made a habit of moving messages between folders, you can speed up the process by clicking the Move to Folder button. When you click the Move to Folder button, you see a list of the last ten folders to which you've moved items. Click the name of a folder on the list, and your message is zapped directly to the folder of your choice.

Using the Sent Items folder

Outlook stores in the Sent Items folder a copy of every message you send unless you tell it to do otherwise. You can review and reread the messages you've sent by looking in the Sent Items folder. To get there, click the My Shortcuts divider on the Outlook bar and then click the Sent Items icon. The same collection of views is available in the Sent Items folder as is available in the Inbox or any other mail folder (*see also* "Using and Choosing E-Mail Views," later in this part).

Printing E-Mail Messages

Printing your e-mail messages is a quaint but sometimes convenient way to deal with the messages you send and receive. Now and then you run across someone who won't read stuff from a screen; they accept only ink on paper. No kidding. Some bosses out there even have assistants type up their voice mail messages; I've seen it. Someday those types will go the way of the dinosaur, and we'll read all our mail on little screens built into our sunglasses while we sit on the beach. Until then, you may have to print your e-mail messages from time to time.

Printing an individual message

 You can print the text of a message you're reading in Outlook by clicking the Print button on the toolbar. The Print button sends your message directly to the printer — without opening a Print dialog box to offer you some choices about what kind of paper to print on or which printer to use (if you're using a network with more than one printer). To see your range of choices before you print, choose File⇔Print (or press Ctrl+P). The principles of printing are the same in all Outlook modules, so *see also* the directions given in "Printing a basic calendar" in Part III for more details.

Printing a list of messages

You can print a list of messages while viewing the contents of your Inbox, Outbox, Sent Items folder, or any mail folder you create. Follow these steps while viewing the list you want to print:

1. Choose File⇔Print (or press Ctrl+P) to open the Print dialog box.

2. Select Table Style from the Print Style list.

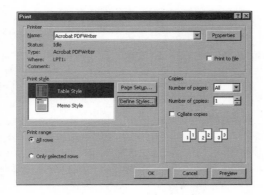

3. Choose other print options, such as the number of copies and which pages to print.

4. Click OK. Your messages are then printed.

Outlook prints whatever message titles are shown in the information viewer when you call up the Print command. If you're in Unread Messages view, for example, only the unread messages are printed. To print your entire list of messages, you have to switch to a view, such as Messages view, that includes all your messages.

Sending and Receiving Online Mail

If you use Outlook to send mail to online services, such as the Microsoft Network or CompuServe, or through an Internet service provider (ISP) you reach by using your telephone line, your outgoing messages are stored in the Outbox until you choose

Tools⇨Send/Receive⇨All Accounts (or press F5) or click the Send/Receive button on the toolbar. Your messages are then dispatched to your online service and sent on to your recipient.

Accessing the Outbox

To view or edit a message that's still stored in your Outbox, follow these steps:

1. Press Ctrl+Shift+O to see the list of messages in your Outbox.

2. Double-click in the Outbox the title of the message you want to view or edit to open the message for editing.

3. Read the message and make any changes you want.

4. Click the Send button (or press Alt+S) to close the Message form and return to a view of your Outbox.

The titles of messages that are ready to be sent appear in italicized text. If you see a message in the Outbox whose title is not italicized, that message isn't sent until you open the message (by double-clicking it) and then click the Send button (or press Alt+S). Messages in the Outbox stay there until you choose Tools⇨ Send and Receive (or press F5).

Checking for new mail

If you use an online service like CompuServe or the Microsoft Network for your e-mail, you have to tell Outlook to pick up the phone and log on to the service. When you do that, Outlook sends the messages you've created and collects the messages sent to you.

To check for new messages, follow these steps:

1. Choose Tools⇨Send and Receive⇨All Accounts (or press F5).

2. The Delivering Messages dialog box appears and remains on the screen until Outlook has checked messages on all your services.

To exchange messages with online services, you have to set up Outlook to use each service. *See also* "Setting up online services," later in this part.

Press F5 to check for new messages on any and all online services you've set up to communicate with Outlook.

Creating personal distribution lists and groups

When you repeatedly send e-mail to the same group of people, you can save lots of time by creating a list that contains the addresses of all the people in the group. Then, when you send your message, rather than enter the name of each person on your list, you only have to enter the name of the list.

Outlook 2000 comes in two different versions: Corporate and Internet Mail Only. You can tell which one you have by checking the Tools menu. If you have a Tools⇨ Services command, you have the Corporate version and can create personal distribution lists.

The Internet Mail Only version of Outlook 2000 doesn't have a Tools⇨Services command, and it doesn't have personal distribution lists. However, it does enable you to create *groups,* which are similar to personal distribution lists. You can tell that you have the Internet Mail Only version of Outlook 2000 if you have a Tools⇨Accounts command. I wish that Microsoft had created a less confusing arrangement for all this stuff, but that's how it is.

Follow these steps to create a personal distribution list:

1. Choose Tools⇨Address Book to open the Address Book dialog box.

2. Choose File⇨New Entry to open the New Entry dialog box.

3. Scroll to the bottom of the Entry Type box and click Personal Distribution List. Make sure that the space at the bottom of the dialog box that says *Put this entry in the* contains the words *Personal Address Book.*

4. Click OK to open the New Personal Distribution List Properties dialog box.

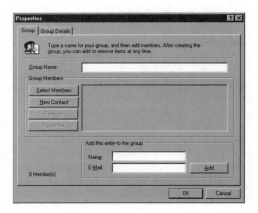

5. Enter in the Name box a name for your new personal distribution list.

6. Click Select Members to open the Edit Members dialog box.

7. Double-click the name of each person you want to include on your personal distribution list. As you double-click each name, the names you choose are copied in the Personal Distribution List box on the right side of the Edit Members dialog box.

8. Click OK after you've finished adding all the names you want to include on your personal distribution list.

If you have the Internet Mail Only version of Outlook 2000, follow these steps to create groups:

1. Choose Tools⇨Address Book to open the Address Book dialog box.

2. Click the New Group button to open the Group Properties dialog box.

3. Enter a name for your new group in the Group Name box.

4. Click the Select Members button to open the Select Group Members dialog box.

5. Double-click the name of each person you want to include in your group. As you double-click each name, the names you choose are copied in the Members box on the right side of the Select Group Members dialog box.

6. Click OK when you've finished adding all the names you want to include in your group.

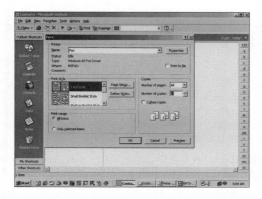

Whenever you want to send a message to everyone in one of your groups or on your personal distribution lists, just type in the To box of your message the name you gave the list in Step 3. You can have as many groups or personal distribution lists as you want. You can also create a group or list a member of another group or list. For example, you can have a list named Vice Presidents for all the VPs in your company and have a list named Senior Management for all those folks. If you make the Vice Presidents list a member of the Senior Management list, you only have to add new vice presidents to the Vice Presidents list; they automatically become a part of the Senior Management list.

Marking remote mail

If you get lots of mail, chances are that some of what you get is important and some isn't so important. When you're at your desk at home or at the office, weeding out unimportant messages is not a big problem. If you need to keep up with important e-mail on your laptop while you're traveling, however, you may not have time to wade through the unimportant stuff.

The Remote Mail feature dials your online service and shows you the subject of the messages waiting for you. You can mark the messages that you think are important and have Outlook get just the messages you marked. Time is money, especially when you're checking your e-mail over a long-distance telephone connection.

Follow these steps to use Remote Mail to pick and choose your messages:

1. Click the Inbox icon on the Outlook bar to switch to the Inbox (if you're not already there).

2. Choose Tools⇨Remote Mail⇨Connect to open the Remote Mail dialog box.

3. Click the name of the online service on which you want to see the titles of your waiting messages. A check mark appears next to the names of the services you select.

4. Click Next to open the Remote Connection Wizard dialog box.

5. Click the button that says Do Only the Following. A line for each message service you choose appears in the box that says something like Retrieve New Message Headers Via the Microsoft Network. Be sure that a check mark appears next to each service you want to check.

6. Click Finish to start the Remote Mail session. The Remote Mail status box remains on-screen until the session is complete.

7. When the Remote Mail session is complete, the titles of any messages you have waiting on your online service appear in your Inbox with a special icon, indicating that the message is still at the online service, waiting for you to retrieve it. You can't read messages until you retrieve them. A new toolbar, called Remote, also appears.

8. Click each message you want to retrieve, and then click the Mark to Retrieve button on the Remote toolbar. A second icon appears next to each message you mark to retrieve.

9. Click the Connect button to open the Remote Connection Wizard dialog box again.

10. Check to see that a check mark is next to the name of the service from which you want to retrieve messages. Normally, the last service you used is still checked.

11. Click Next to move to the next step of the Remote Connection Wizard.

12. Click Finish to start the Remote Mail session. The Remote Mail status box remains on-screen until all your messages are retrieved.

13. Your messages appear in the Inbox. Double-click the names of the messages you want to read.

As you can see, the Remote Mail Wizard is somewhat time-consuming for something that's supposed to save you time. If you get large amounts of e-mail, you'll find Remote Mail necessary from time to time. Normally, however, you're better off just choosing Tools⇨Send and Receive (or pressing F5).

Reading attachments

Whenever you receive a message with a file attached (*see also* "Attaching files to your messages," earlier in this part), you have to open the attachment before you can read whatever is in the attachment. No problemo:

1. Double-click the name of the message that has an attachment you want to read. The Message form opens.

2. An icon in the body of the message represents each file attached to the message. Just double-click the icon to open the attachment; double-clicking the icon also launches the program that created the message.

An even faster way to get a peek at the contents of a file attached to a message you receive is to right-click the icon for the attachment and choose QuickView from the shortcut menu. Although you can't make changes to a document when you're using the QuickView feature, you can get a glimpse of what the attachment is about.

Setting up online services

Before you can use Outlook to exchange e-mail through an online service — such as CompuServe, America Online, or the Microsoft

Network — or through an Internet service provider — such as Netcom or AT&T WorldNet — you have to set up Outlook to work with that particular service.

If you work in a large organization that uses Microsoft Exchange Server for its e-mail system, your system administrators will set up the Outlook 2000 Corporate version for you. They probably don't want you setting up online services on the copy of Outlook 2000 on your desktop, so I don't get into it in this book. You can still send e-mail to people on online services, like CompuServe or AOL, by typing their address in the To box of your message.

If you're using Outlook 2000 somewhere other than on a large corporate network, you should use the Outlook 2000 Internet Mail Only version. The Internet Mail Only version enables you to set up e-mail accounts to work with most online services and Internet service providers. Although the method you use to set up any service is somewhat similar, the exact details differ, and those differences are important. Before you begin to set up Outlook e-mail accounts, it's a good idea to check with the tech-support people from your online service so that you understand the details.

After you get the skinny from your online service, follow these steps to set up e-mail accounts on the Outlook 2000 Internet Mail Only version:

1. Choose Tools⇨Accounts.

2. Click the Add button and then choose Mail from the shortcut menu to start the Internet Connection Wizard.

3. Follow the prompts in the Internet Connection Wizard and enter the information provided by your online service or Internet service provider.

Using and Choosing E-Mail Views

One of the real benefits of Outlook is the variety of ways in which you can sort and arrange your collection of messages, as well as the several different ways you can look at what's in your messages. Your Outlook folders can serve as your filing system as well as your electronic mailbox.

You have many different arrangements you can use to view your e-mail messages. If you don't like the view you have, you can choose View⇨Current View and pick a new view.

Follow these steps to choose a new view:

✦ **Messages view:** A plain-vanilla list of your messages. The titles of unread messages are shown in boldface, whereas messages you've read are shown in a normal typeface.

✦ **Messages with AutoPreview:** Shows you the first few lines of all your unread messages.

✦ **By Follow-Up Flag:** Shows a list of your messages according to which kind of flag you've assigned to each message.

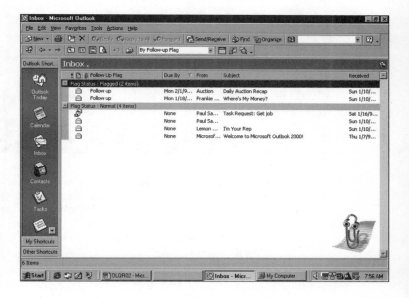

✦ **Last Seven Days:** A list of messages you've received within the past seven days.

✦ **Flagged for Next Seven Days:** Shows only flagged messages with due dates scheduled within the next week.

✦ **By Conversation Topic:** Organizes your messages by subject.

✦ **By Sender:** Groups your messages according to who sent the message.

✦ **Unread Messages:** Shows only unread messages. After you read a message, this view no longer appears.

+ **Sent To:** Sorts messages according to the name of the person
  it's sent to. In your Inbox, most messages are sent to you, so it
  makes little sense to use this view in the Inbox. In your Sent
  Items folder, however, you can use Sent To view to organize
  your outgoing messages according to the person to whom
  each message is sent.

+ **Message Timeline:** Shows you a diagram with your messages
  organized by the time they were sent or received. You can
  click the icon shown for any message and see that message.

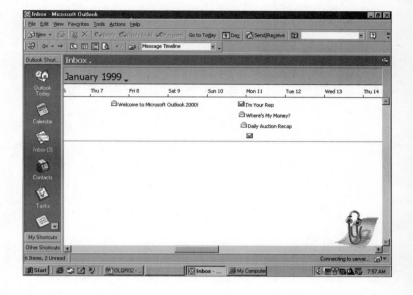

Part III

Calendar

You never have enough time in the day, so there's no sense in wasting precious minutes figuring out what to do next. The Microsoft Outlook Calendar can help you organize appointments, holidays, and recurring events. You can also get Outlook to remind you about a meeting early enough to be sure that you get there on time.

In this part . . .

- ✔ **Changing an appointment**
- ✔ **Deleting an item from your calendar**
- ✔ **Reviewing your calendar**
- ✔ **Scheduling an appointment**
- ✔ **Scheduling an event**
- ✔ **Scheduling and rescheduling a recurring appointment**
- ✔ **Sharing your calendar**
- ✔ **Printing your schedule**

Changing an Appointment

What? You say that your schedule never changes? You say that you never need to change your schedule? Well, I, for one, don't believe you. The world's pace is just too fast for anyone's schedule to last for even a short time without modification. Fortunately, Outlook makes its easy to change appointments.

Changing an appointment by using drag-and-drop

Changing the starting time or the date of an appointment is just a matter of using the drag-and-drop technique. Follow these steps to pick up the appointment and slide it to the date or time you want:

1. Click the appointment in Calendar view.

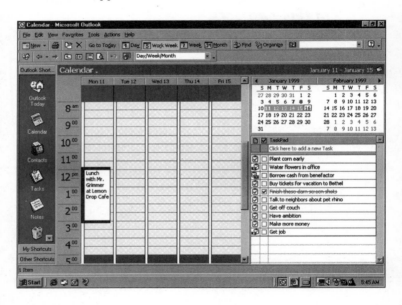

2. Place the mouse pointer over the blue bar; the mouse pointer turns into a little four-headed arrow.

3. Press the mouse button, drag the appointment to the new time or date, and release the button.

If you want to change the date of an appointment but not the time, the easiest method is to choose a view of your calendar that includes both the original appointment date and the date you want to assign to the appointment. To change the time, for example, switch to One-Day view and slide the appointment to its new time slot. To change an appointment to a date later in the same month, choose 31-Day view and drag the appointment to the new date. You can always double-click the appointment to open it, of course, and then change everything (***see also*** "Reopening an appointment to change it," a little later in this part).

Changing the length of an appointment

When you're looking at One-Day view in your calendar, your appointments are shown as boxes of different sizes, depending on the length of the appointment. If you want to shorten or lengthen an appointment, just use your mouse to drag the border of the box that represents the appointment to make the appointment smaller or bigger.

Follow these steps to shorten or lengthen an appointment:

1. Click the appointment.

2. Move the mouse pointer over the line at the bottom of the appointment.

3. Drag the bottom line down to make the appointment time longer; drag the bottom line up to make the appointment shorter.

Another method is to drag the top line up or down, but bear in mind that dragging the top line changes both the appointment's length *and* its starting time.

Dragging the box to change the length of an appointment is the easiest way to go if all your appointments begin and end on the hour and half-hour. If your appointments don't start on the hour or half-hour, you can fine-tune the length of an appointment by opening the appointment and typing the starting and ending times you want (***see also*** "Shortening appointments to less than 30 minutes," a little later in this part).

You also can use the drag-and-drop method when you change the length of events. To change the length of an event, click the 31-Day button to switch to Monthly view in your calendar and then just drag the line at the left or right end of the banner that represents an event to make an event longer or shorter.

Reopening an appointment to change it

Drag-and-drop isn't the ticket for changing appointment times when you can't view enough of the calendar to see both the original date and the rescheduled date. In that case, all you can do is reopen the appointment and change the particulars.

To reopen an appointment, follow these steps:

1. Double-click the appointment.

2. Click in the first Start Time block and enter the date you want to assign to your appointment.

3. Press the Tab key and enter the new appointment time in the text box (if you have a new time).

4. If necessary, make any other changes in the appointment by clicking the information you want to change and entering the revised information over it.

5. Click the Save and Close button (or press Alt+S).

Shortening appointments to less than 30 minutes

When you use the drag-and-drop method to change the length of appointments, you can make appointments begin and end only on the hour and at 30 minutes after the hour. When you have appointments that you need to begin and end at other times, you have to open the appointment and enter the times you want, just as you did when you first created the appointment, like this:

1. Double-click the appointment.

2. To change the time the appointment begins, click the Start Time box and type the time you want.

3. To change the time the appointment ends, click the End Time box and type the time you want. You also can change any other details about the appointment while the Appointment form is open.

4. Click the Save and Close button (or press Alt+S).

Remember, when you enter times in Outlook, you don't have to be particular about punctuation. For example, when you type **5p**, Outlook understands it to be 5:00 p.m. and automatically converts the time to the proper format. Dates are even easier to enter; just enter **next Wed**, and Outlook converts it to the date.

Deleting an Item from Your Calendar

Deleting items in Outlook is *intuitive,* which means that you probably can figure out how to do it without my telling you. Of course, I tell you anyway:

1. Click the appointment you want to delete.

 2. Click the Delete button on the toolbar (or press Delete).

If you want to delete several appointments at one time, hold down the Ctrl key while clicking each appointment you want to delete. Then press Delete.

Printing Your Schedule

You may want to print a copy of your schedule to carry around as a reminder, or you can print your appointments for someone else to use. Outlook can print your appointment calendar in dozens of different formats to fit your preference.

If you use a paper planner and want to manage your schedule with Outlook and print it to use in your paper planner, you can create pages that fit in several popular planners, including

✦ Day Runner

✦ Day-Timer

+ FiloFax

+ Franklin Day Planner

You also can print a tiny copy of your schedule that's small enough to carry around in your billfold or a full-page calendar to post on a wall.

About the Print dialog box

 When you click the print button on the tool bar (or press Ctrl+P), Outlook prepares to print a copy of whatever is on-screen by opening the Print dialog box. The Print dialog box changes the way it looks depending on which Outlook module you're using, which view you've chosen, and which items are in the view you've selected (if any).

The Print Style list in the Print dialog box shows you a collection of tiny diagrams of different ways you can have your information arranged on the page. Click the diagram that looks the way you want your page to look.

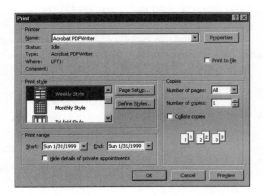

The Page Setup button next to the Print Style box enables you to tell Outlook what kind of paper to use and other details about printing in the style you've chosen. Choices you make after clicking the Page Setup button apply only to the style you selected from the Print Style list.

The Define Styles button enables you to create your own styles and give each new style a name you choose. After you create a style, the name and a diagram of the style appear on the Print Style list.

The Print Range box enables you to tell Outlook how much information to include on the pages you print. In Calendar, you have to enter a range of dates. In all the other Outlook modules, you choose All Rows or Only Selected Rows.

The Preview button enables you to see exactly what your pages will look like when you print them. You save a great deal of time if you preview your pages before printing them, because you can be sure that your pages look the way you want before wasting time and paper on printed copies. Previewing takes only a second.

About Print styles

Each style you see on the Print Styles list gives you a different collection of choices about what appears on the pages you print. You may want to create entirely new styles to fit your needs. Perhaps you print a copy of your calendar every month to post on your wall and you print another monthly calendar to carry around in your date book. You can create special styles for each one and save the trouble of having to enter all the particulars about each calendar's paper size, paper type, page layout, and so on every month.

 To create a new Print style, follow these steps:

1. Click the Print button on the toolbar (or press Ctrl+P) to open the Print dialog box.

2. In the Print dialog box, choose Daily, Weekly, or Monthly from the Print Style list.

3. Click the Define Styles button to open the Define Styles dialog box.

4. Choose the style on which you want to base your new style.

5. Click the Copy button to open the Page Setup dialog box.

6. Click the Style Name text box and enter the name you want to give your new style.

7. Choose from the Format tab the options you want, including layout. The options that are available to you depend on the style you chose as a basis for your new style in Step 4.

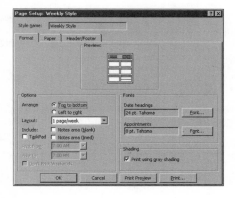

8. Click the Paper tab in the Page Setup dialog box.

9. From the Type list, choose the type of paper you're using.

10. From the Size list, choose the size of paper you're using.

11. If you want any particular information to print at the top or bottom of the page, click the Header/Footer tab and enter what you want to print.

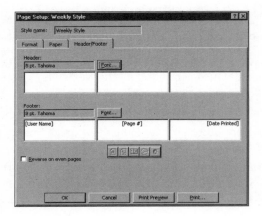

12. Click the Print Preview button to see what your new style looks like.

13. Click OK to close the Page Setup dialog box.

14. Click Close to close the Define Print Styles dialog box.

15. Click OK to print your schedule.

After you define a style, its name shows up on the Print Styles list in the Print dialog box, so you only have to choose your style and click OK.

If you plan to print in a certain style only once, you don't need to create a whole new style; just click the Page Setup button and change the style to meet your needs.

Creating a billfold-size calendar

One handy calendar style is a tiny billfold-size calendar that contains your schedule, a convenience calendar, and a list of your tasks.

Follow these steps to create a Billfold calendar you can use every day:

1. Click the Calendar icon on the Outlook bar, if you're not in the Calendar module.

2. Choose View⇨Current View⇨Day/Week/Month.

 3. Click either the Day, Work Week, or Week button on the toolbar.

 4. Click the Print button on the toolbar (or press Ctrl+P) to open the Print dialog box.

5. In the Print dialog box, choose Trifold from the Print Style list.

6. Click the Page Setup button to open the Page Setup dialog box.

7. Click the Paper tab in the Page Setup dialog box.

8. Click Billfold from the Size list.

9. Click OK to close the Page Setup dialog box.

10. Click OK to print your schedule.

 The Billfold style prints your schedule in an area about the size of a dollar bill, so if you print on normal-size paper, you have to take a pair of scissors and cut off the excess.

Printing a basic calendar

If you've ever printed anything in Windows, you already know the basics: Put what you want to print on the screen and tell Outlook to print it. More choices are available when you're printing your calendar, but here's the basic method:

1. Click a date within the range of dates you want to print.

 2. Click the Print button on the toolbar (or press Ctrl+P) to open the Print dialog box.

3. In the Print Style group, choose Daily, Weekly, Monthly, Trifold, Memo, or any other style you want that may be available in the Print Style box (*see also* "About Print styles," earlier in this part).

4. In the Print Range box, set the range of dates you want to print.

5. Click OK.

Printing a calendar to use in your planner

If you're printing pages of your calendar to use in a planner book, such as Day Runner or Franklin Day Planner, you can take advantage of some of the print styles that come with Outlook.

Follow these steps to set up your pages for a commercial planner:

1. Click the Calendar icon on the Outlook bar, if you're not in the Calendar module.

2. Choose View⇨Current View⇨Day/Week/Month.

3. Click the Print button on the toolbar (or press Ctrl+P) to open the Print dialog box.

4. In the Print dialog box, choose Daily, Weekly, or Monthly from the Print Style list.

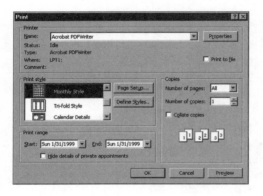

5. Click the Define Styles button to open the Define Print Styles dialog box.

6. Click the Edit button to open the Page Setup dialog box.

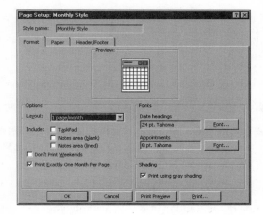

7. Click the Paper tab in the Page Setup dialog box.

8. From the Type list, choose the type of paper you're using.

You can buy special paper for most types of planners from the people who manufacture the planners. If you're using paper from the original manufacturer, such as Day Runner or Franklin Day Planner, choose Custom on the Type list.

Avery makes filler paper that fits some popular planners. Look for it at your local office supply store. If you're using Avery paper, choose the Avery paper type listed on the Type list.

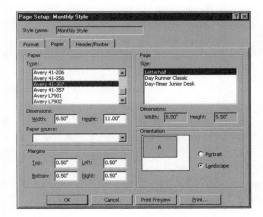

9. Choose from the Page Size list the type of planner (such as Day Runner Running Mate or Franklin Day Planner) for which you're printing pages.

10. Click OK to close the Page Setup dialog box.

11. Click Close to close the Define Print Styles dialog box.

12. Click OK to print your schedule.

After you set up the page by using the Define Print Styles dialog box, you get the same type of page every time you print your schedule.

Printing a calendar to hang on a wall

You can also print a calendar that fills a whole sheet of paper suitable for hanging on your wall or taping to the fridge. You can use paper as large as 8¹/₂-by-14-inch legal paper. Follow these steps:

1. Click the Calendar icon on the Outlook bar, if you're not in the Calendar module.

2. Choose View⇨Current View⇨Day/Week/Month.

3. Click the Print button on the toolbar (or press Ctrl+P) to open the Print dialog box.

4. In the Print dialog box, choose Daily, Weekly, or Monthly from the Print Style list.

5. Click the Page Setup button to open the Page Setup dialog box.

6. Click the Paper tab in the Page Setup dialog box.

7. Choose the paper size you're using from *both* the Type and Size lists (either Letter or Legal).

8. Click OK to close the Page Setup dialog box.

9. Click OK to print your schedule.

You have literally hundreds of combinations of paper sizes, styles, and layouts to use for printing your calendar. You can't hurt anything by experimenting with different sizes and trying new things.

For now, you can't print a 6- or 12-month calendar on a single page in Outlook. Although this task seems like a simple thing to do, Outlook isn't up to it just yet.

Reviewing Your Calendar

You enter appointments in Outlook so that you can remember them later. To use your appointment list in that way, you have to at least look at your list of appointments. Outlook enables you to view your list in dozens of ways (an Outlook *view* is a way of presenting information in the arrangement you need). Outlook comes with six different views, and you can create your own views. This section describes the views you get the first time you use Outlook.

Basic Calendar views

When you first use Outlook, you have a half-dozen preprogrammed views from which to choose. Although you can add views to your heart's content in any Outlook module, you can go a long way with the views Outlook starts with. Here's the view lineup:

✦ **Day/Week/Month:** Looks like a calendar. Buttons on the toolbar enable you to choose between viewing your appointments for one day, a week, or a whole month. You'll probably use this view more often than any other.

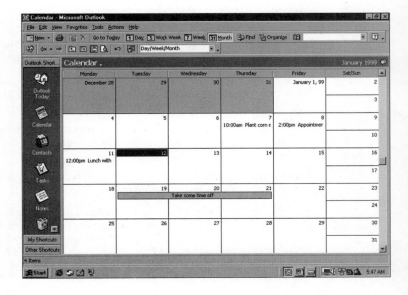

✦ **Active Appointments:** A list of appointments that are coming up soon. Although this view shows some of the same appointments as Day/Week/Month view, this view also shows you information about each appointment and enables you to sort the list according to the location or subject you entered when you created the appointment.

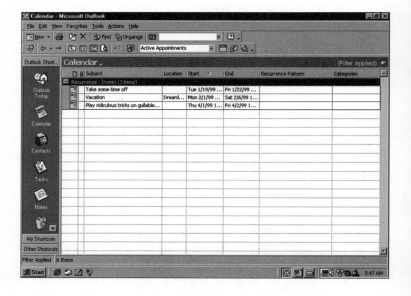

✦ **Events:** A list that shows you only items you've designated as All Day Events (*see also* "Scheduling an Event," later in this part).

✦ **Annual Events:** Shows only the list of events you've made into recurring events that happen yearly. You can enter holidays and anniversaries as annual events.

✦ **Recurring Appointments:** Lists all appointments and events you've set as recurring appointments.

✦ **By Category:** Groups your appointments according to the category you've assigned to each appointment. Grouped views work the same way in all Outlook modules (*see also* "Using grouped views," in Part V).

Another popular way to view your upcoming appointments is to click the Outlook Today icon on the Outlook bar. As its name suggests, Outlook Today pulls together everything you're doing today — appointments, tasks, and messages — and displays it all on a single page. You can print your Outlook Today page by clicking the Print button on the toolbar or by pressing Ctrl+P.

Changing the amount of time displayed

Outlook enables you to choose from several calendar styles. Some styles show a bigger calendar with fewer dates, and some styles show a smaller calendar with more dates but include no notes about what's scheduled on a certain date. The Date Navigator is a small calendar that enables you to see your schedule for the date of your choice by simply clicking the date with your mouse.

To use the Date Navigator, follow these steps:

   1. Switch to the Calendar module by clicking the Calendar icon on the Outlook bar to make your calendar appear.

   2. Choose View⇨Current View⇨Day/Week/Month.

   3. Click either the Day, Work Week, or Week button on the toolbar.

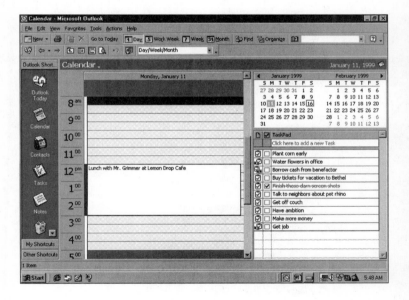

The little calendar in the upper-right corner is the Date Navigator. The rest of the screen shows your appointments for the current week (or the days you've clicked in the Date Navigator). To see what's scheduled for a different date, just click the date on the Date Navigator.

Customizing the TaskPad

The Day/Week/Month view of your calendar includes a snippet of your task list (**see also** Part IV). Although the TaskPad shows the exact same items you see if you switch to the Tasks module, the information you see is less detailed. I find it handy to have the TaskPad available when I'm looking at my calendar so that I can view the things I have to do at certain times in addition to the things I can do at any time. Another benefit of the TaskPad is that when I print my calendar, I can also print my tasks.

You can view or print tasks from your calendar, but you can't view or print calendar items from the Tasks module. If you need to view and print both at the same time, stay in the Calendar module.

You can set up the TaskPad to show your tasks in several ways. Follow these steps to choose the TaskPad style you prefer:

1. Click the Calendar icon on the Outlook bar, if you're not in the Calendar module.

2. Choose View⇨Current View⇨Day/Week/Month.

3. Choose View⇨TaskPad View and pick the type of TaskPad view you want. The TaskPad uses the same views as the Tasks module (*see also* Part IV).

Going to one date

The calendar in Outlook can schedule appointments hundreds or even thousands of years from now. In case you're concerned, Outlook has no problem with the year 2000 (or the year 3000 or 4000, for that matter). Because you have so many years to work with, you need a quick way to make the calendar show the date you're thinking about. These steps show the quick way:

1. Click the Calendar icon on the Outlook bar, if you're not in the Calendar module. When you switch to the Calendar module from another module, Outlook always shows you the current date.

2. Choose <u>V</u>iew⇨Current <u>V</u>iew⇨Day/Week/Month.

3. Choose <u>G</u>o⇨Go to Dat<u>e</u> (or press Ctrl+G).

4. Enter the date you want, such as **12/25/2098**, or **Christmas 2098**, or **1 year from now**, or even **100 years from now**. Outlook figures out what you mean.

5. Click OK to make the calendar display the date you've chosen.

6. Click the Go to Today button on the toolbar to return to today's date.

Resizing parts of Day/Week/Month view

The one- and seven-day views in Day/Week/Month view fill the screen with three parts you can resize by dragging the borders with your mouse.

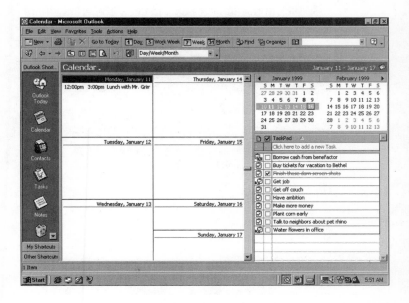

If you want to give the Date Navigator a little more space, drag the gray borderline just below or to the left of the Date Navigator until it's the size you want. You can make the Date Navigator take up the whole screen if you want.

Dragging the border to the left of the TaskPad changes the amount of space the TaskPad occupies. When you change the size of one element of Day/Week/Month view, the other elements are either resized or disappear to compensate.

Scheduling an Appointment

Although Outlook gives you lots of choices for entering details about your appointments, you have to enter only two things: what and when. Everything else is optional.

If you want to schedule two appointments at the same time, Outlook subtly warns you with a banner at the top of the form that says *Conflicts with another appointment,* although nothing stops you from scheduling yourself to be in two places at one time. Just to be safe, look at the schedule for the time you are scheduling first:

1. Click the Calendar icon on the Outlook bar, if you're not in the Calendar module.

2. Click the New Appointment button on the toolbar.

3. Click in the Subject box and enter something there to help you to remember what the appointment is about.

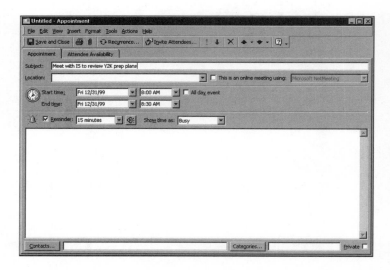

4. Click in the Location box and enter the location, if you want. If you know the location, enter it there so that you don't forget.

5. In the Start Time boxes, enter the date and time when the appointment begins.

6. In the End Time boxes, enter the date and time when the appointment ends. If you ignore the End Time boxes, Outlook creates a 30-minute appointment.

7. If you want Outlook to remind you of your appointment, click the Reminder box.

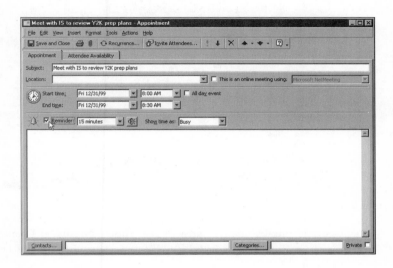

8. Enter a category of your choice in the Categories box.

9. Click the Save and Close button on the toolbar.

If you're on a network and don't want others to know about your appointment, click the Private box in the lower-right corner of the dialog box.

Scheduling an Event

An *event* is a type of calendar entry much like an appointment, except that it lasts all day and isn't associated with a particular hour of the day. Holidays are events. You can schedule more than one event for the same day; for example, if your birthday falls on Christmas Day, you can schedule two events for December 25. (You still get only one present, however.) You can also schedule a convention or business trip as an event and then continue scheduling appointments on the event day. Events also look different on your calendar: Each event appears as a gray banner on the calendar day on which it's scheduled.

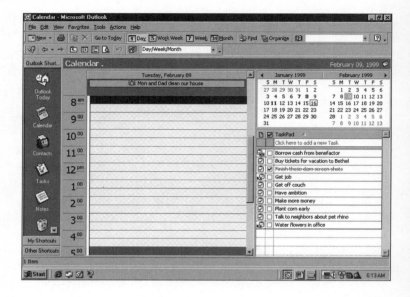

You use exactly the same steps to enter events as you use to enter appointments, except that you also check the All Day Event box (*see also* "Scheduling an Appointment," earlier in this part).

Scheduling a Recurring Appointment

Some appointments keep coming back like a bad penny. Your Monday morning staff meeting or Wednesday night bowling league roll around every week unchanged (except for your bowling score), so why enter the appointment over and over? Just call it a *recurring appointment*.

To create a recurring appointment, follow these steps:

1. Click the New Appointment button on the left end of the toolbar to open the New Appointment form.

2. Click in the Subject box and enter the subject.

3. Click in the Location box and enter the location.

4. Click the Recurrence button on the toolbar (or press Ctrl+G) to make the Appointment Recurrence dialog box appear.

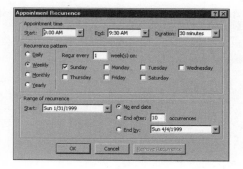

5. Click the Start text box and enter the starting time.

6. Click the End text box and enter the ending time. (Don't worry about the Duration box; Outlook calculates the duration for you. On the other hand, you can just enter the duration and let Outlook fill in the missing end time.)

7. In the Recurrence Pattern box, click the Daily, Weekly, Monthly, or Yearly option button to select how often the appointment recurs.

8. In the next part of the Recurrence Pattern box, choose how often the appointment occurs. The recurrence pattern looks different depending on whether you chose Daily, Weekly, Monthly, or Yearly in Step 7. The preceding figure shows the Weekly Recurrence Pattern box.

  • If you chose a Yearly pattern, choose something like the last Sunday in January.

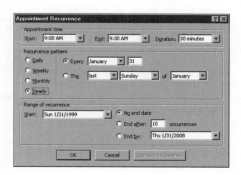

- If you chose a Weekly recurrence pattern, choose something like every Sunday.

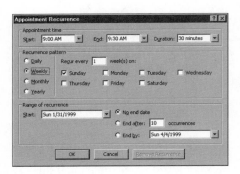

- If you chose a Daily pattern, choose something like every eighth day or even every day.

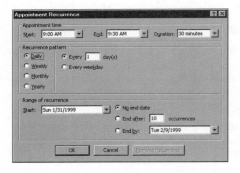

9. In the Range of Recurrence box, enter the first occurrence in the Start box.

10. Choose when the appointments will end. If you want the appointment to repeat indefinitely, you don't have to do anything; No End Date is checked by default if you don't choose something else. Don't worry about the box labeled End After 10 Occurrences; the button with the dot in it tells you which choice you've picked. After you create a recurring appointment with no end date, your appointment recurs forever until you reopen the Appointment form and change the pattern or delete the appointment.

11. Click OK.

12. Click the Save and Close button (or press Alt+S).

A quick way to enter the date when a recurring appointment will end is to enter something like **two years from now** and let Outlook translate that into an actual date. (You may not want to really challenge Outlook by entering *when cows fly.*)

Rescheduling a Recurring Appointment

Outlook treats recurring appointments a little differently from single appointments because what you do to one appointment in a series of recurring appointments may affect later occurrences of that appointment. For example, if you change your regular Wednesday night tennis match to Thursday night in order to compete against players who are weaker or better looking (or both), you're probably changing all your future tennis dates. If you're changing your match just one Wednesday night in order to see your child's school play, you're just changing one appointment in a series.

Follow these steps to reschedule a recurring appointment:

1. Double-click the appointment you want to change. The Open Recurring Item dialog box appears.

2. Choose whether you want to change just the occurrence you clicked or the whole series.

3. Click OK to reopen the Appointment form.

4. Change the date, start time, recurrence pattern, or any other details of the appointment on the Appointment form, just as you first entered the appointment (*see also* "Scheduling an Appointment," earlier in the part).

5. Click the <u>S</u>ave and Close button (or press Alt+S).

You can still change individual occurrences of a recurring appointment by dragging the appointment to a different time. When you do, Outlook asks whether you want to change only this occurrence. If you want to change only one occurrence, click OK.

Sharing Your Calendar

The only thing that wastes more time than going to meetings is calling people to find out when they can go to meetings. Outlook 2000 enables you to share your calendar with other Outlook 2000 users so that you can settle on a meeting time by checking another person's calendar yourself. You have to install an option named Net Folders from the Outlook 2000 CD-ROM in order to share your Outlook folders with someone else. If you want to know more about sharing folders with Outlook 2000, see the large, luxurious version of this book, *Microsoft Outlook 2000 For Dummies* (IDG Books Worldwide, Inc.), which features an entire chapter devoted to Net Folders.

Part IV

Tasks

All those little tasks I have to do every day have a way of slipping off my radar screen until just after I need to do them. That's why I like having a simple tool for tracking what needs to be done and when. The Tasks module enables me to deal with simple things quickly, yet it's designed to also help me keep track of fairly complex activities.

You also can use Outlook to manage tasks in cooperation with your colleagues at work. To do that, however, your company must be running another Microsoft program, Microsoft Exchange Server. I don't know whether your company uses Exchange Server, so I don't want to confuse you. Therefore, I minimize the discussion of features that require Exchange Server, such as responding to task requests and sending status reports. You get plenty of mileage from the Outlook Tasks module by itself.

In this part . . .

- ✔ **Attaching a file to a task item**
- ✔ **Changing the appearance of your task list**
- ✔ **Creating a new task**
- ✔ **Creating a recurring task**
- ✔ **Creating a regenerating task**
- ✔ **Deleting a task**
- ✔ **Modifying an existing task**
- ✔ **Printing tasks**
- ✔ **Sending a task to someone else**
- ✔ **Setting the color of overdue or completed tasks**
- ✔ **Skipping a recurring task once**
- ✔ **Tracking the progress of a task**

Attaching a File to a Task Item

You can include word processing documents, spreadsheets, or any other type of file in a task by making the document an *attachment*. For example, if you've had a bad day and enter **Update Résumé** as your new task, you can link your résumé to the task to find the résumé faster when you're ready to update it.

To link a task to an attachment, follow these steps:

1. Double-click the task to open the Task form.

 2. Click the Insert File button on the toolbar to open the Insert File dialog box.

3. Choose from the list of files in the Insert File dialog box the file you want to attach.

4. Click Insert to close the dialog box and return to the Task form.

5. Click the Save and Close button (or press Alt+S).

The process of attaching files to your tasks is much like the process for attaching files to any other Outlook item. (*See also* "Attaching files to your messages," in Part II.) When you delete a task that has a file attached, only the task — not the file — is deleted.

Changing the Appearance of Your Task List

Task lists are just that: lists of tasks. You don't typically need fancy layouts when you choose a view. You just need a list that contains the information you want. To switch between views, choose

View⇨Current View, and then pick the view you want to use.
Here's a list of the views that come with Outlook right out of
the box:

✦ **Simple List:** Just the facts — the names you gave each task
and the due date you assigned (if you assigned one). Simple
List view makes it easy to add new tasks and to mark old ones
as complete. However, you don't see any extra information.

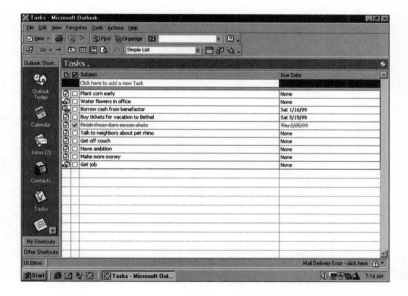

✦ **Detailed List:** A little more, uh, detailed than Simple List view.
It's really the same information, plus the status of the tasks,
the percentage completed of each task, and whatever categories you may have assigned to your tasks.

✦ **Active List:** Shows you only tasks you haven't finished yet.
After you mark a task as complete — zap! Completed tasks
vanish from Active List view, which helps keep you focused on
your remaining tasks.

✦ **Next Seven Days:** Even more focused than Active List view. Next Seven Days view shows only uncompleted tasks scheduled to be done within the next seven days. It's just right for people who like to live in the moment, or at least within the week.

✦ **Overdue Tasks:** Shows (oops!) tasks you've let slip past the due date you assigned. You ought to finish these up before the boss finds out.

✦ **By Category:** Breaks up your tasks according to the category you've assigned each task. You can open and close categories to focus on the type of tasks you're looking for. For example, you may assign a category of Sales to the sales-related tasks on your list. When you want to focus on sales, use By Category view and click the Sales category.

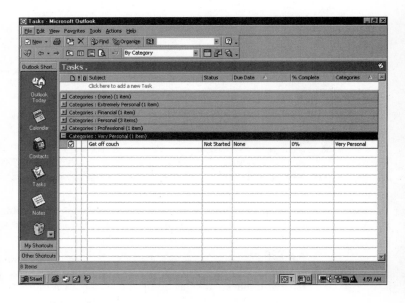

✦ **Assignment:** Lists your tasks in order by the name of the person on whom you've dumped — er, I mean, to whom you've delegated — each task.

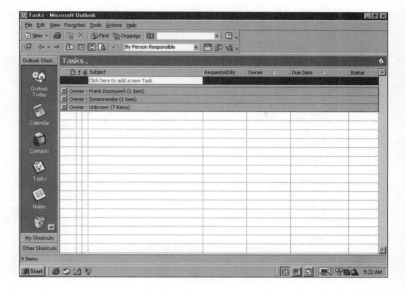

+ **By Person Responsible:** Contains the same information as Assignment view, except that the list is grouped so that you can see the assignments of only one person at a time.

+ **Completed Tasks:** Shows (you guessed it) only tasks you've marked as complete. You don't have to deal with completed tasks anymore, but looking at the list gives you a warm, fuzzy feeling, doesn't it?

+ **Task Timeline:** Draws a picture of when each task is scheduled to begin and end. Seeing a picture of your tasks gives you a better idea of how to fit work into your schedule sensibly.

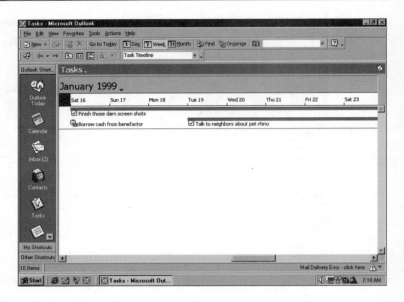

Creating a New Task

Outlook can handle all kinds of high-falutin' information and
details about each task you enter. I find that 90 percent of the time,
I just need to type a quick note to jog my memory. For the other
10 percent, however, I need to go whole hog and keep lots of
information handy about tasks I must do — things like travel
directions and discussion notes.

Creating an abbreviated task quickly

Most times, I need only a word or two to jog my memory about a
task, something like **Call Mom.** I don't need much detailed information about how to do that, so I resort to the fast way:

1. Click the Tasks icon on the Outlook bar to switch to the Tasks
module if you aren't already there.

If you don't see anything that says Click Here to Add a New
Task, switch to a different view of your task list by choosing
View⇨Current View⇨Simple List (**see also** "Choosing a view,"
in Part V).

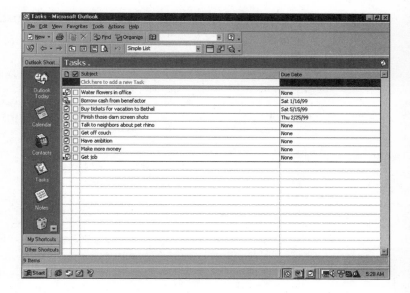

2. Click the text that says Click Here to Add a New Task. This step makes an insertion point (a flashing vertical bar) appear where the words were.

3. Type the name of your task.

4. Press the Enter key to make your new task drop down to join your list of other tasks.

If you're using Calendar, you can use TaskPad, a miniature version of the task list. You can enter tasks in the TaskPad by typing in the box labeled Click Here to Add a New Task.

Creating a detailed task slowly

Suppose that you need to enter more information about your task, such as driving directions, or you want to have Outlook remind you just before the task is due. There is no limit to the information you can add to a task if you go the slow, complete way.

Most of the steps I show you include an "If" to let you know that you can skip the step if you're not interested in saving the type of information it discusses. The only essential element of a task is the name of the task. Everything else is optional.

Follow these steps:

1. Click the Tasks icon on the Outlook bar to switch to the Tasks module if you're not already there.

2. Click the New Task button on the toolbar (or press Ctrl+N) to open a blank New Task form.

3. Type the name of the task in the Subject box.

4. If you want to assign a due date to the task, click the Due Date button; then click the Due Date box and enter the due date. You don't have to be fussy about how you enter the date; Outlook understands **7/4/98, the first Saturday of July,** or **90 days from today** — however you like it.

5. If you want to enter a start date, click the Start Date box and enter a date. Because not all tasks have start dates, you can skip this step if you want.

6. If you want to keep track of the status of a task, click the triangle at the right end of the Status box (the scroll-down button). You have to revise your task as the status of the task progresses (*see also* "Modifying a task the quick, simple way," later in this part).

7. If the task you're entering is unusually important, urgent, or even relatively unimportant, click the scroll-down button at the right end of the Priority box to choose the priority of the task.

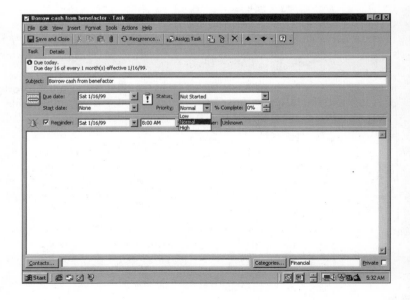

8. If you want to be reminded before the task is due, click the Reminder check box and then click the date box next to it and enter the date on which you want to be reminded. Enter in the time box the time of day you want to activate the reminder.

9. If you want, enter miscellaneous notes and information about this task in the text box.

10. If you want to assign a category to your task, type in the Categories text box the category you want.

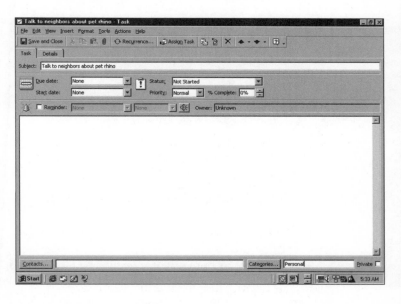

11. Click the Save and Close button (or press Alt+S) to finish.

You can enter quite a bit of detailed information if you use the slow, complete method, but you don't have to use this method all the time. Another advantage of the slow, complete method is that you can use it to create a task when you're using any other Outlook module; just press Ctrl+Shift+K to open the New Task form and then start with Step 3.

Creating a Recurring Task

When tasks have to be done over and over on a regular schedule, set them up as *recurring* tasks. You can designate a task as recurring while you're entering the task the first time.

You also can create a recurring task by reopening the task and following these steps:

1. Double-click the task to open the Task form.

 2. To open the Task Recurrence dialog box, click the Recurrence button on the toolbar of the Task form (or press Ctrl+G).

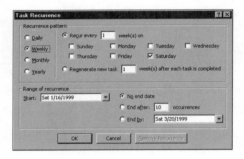

3. Choose the Daily, Weekly, Monthly, or Yearly option to specify how often the task occurs.

4. In the next box to the right, specify how often the appointment occurs, such as **every third day** or **the first Monday of each month.**

5. In the Range of Recurrence area, enter the first occurrence in the Start box.

6. Choose when the appointments will stop (no end date, after a certain number of occurrences, or at a certain date).

7. Click OK to close the Task Recurrence dialog box.

8. Click the Save and Close button (or press Alt+S).

Recurring tasks can be confusing because the Task Recurrence dialog box changes its appearance depending on whether you choose a daily, weekly, monthly, or yearly recurrence pattern. The principles for creating a recurring task are the same as those you use for creating recurring appointments. (*See also* "Scheduling a Recurring Appointment" in Part III.)

Creating a Regenerating Task

Sometimes it doesn't make sense to schedule the next occurrence of a task until you've completed the preceding occurrence. For example, if you get your hair cut every two weeks but you get busy and get one haircut a week late, you still want to wait two weeks for the following haircut. If you use Outlook to schedule your haircuts, set it up as a regenerating task. (If only I could get Outlook to make my hair regenerate as well.) A regenerating task is "getting a haircut every two weeks," and a recurring task is "getting a haircut every Monday."

Follow these steps to create a regenerating task:

1. Double-click the task to open the Task form.

 2. Click the Recurrence button on the toolbar on the Task form (or press Ctrl+G) to open the Task Recurrence dialog box.

3. Click the Regenerate New Task option.

4. Enter the number of months between regenerating the task.

5. Click OK to close the Task Recurrence dialog box.

6. Click the Save and Close button (or press Alt+S).

 I wish that I could schedule tasks to regenerate every few days or every few weeks, but the only choice available in Outlook is to regenerate tasks in full-month increments.

Deleting a Task

Sometimes you change your mind about a task you've assigned yourself and want to delete the task. Deleting tasks is *so* much simpler than getting them done.

Follow these steps to delete a task:

1. Select the task by clicking the Task icon in the first column of the list.

 2. Click the Delete button on the toolbar (or press Ctrl+D).

You'll never know that the task existed.

Modifying an Existing Task

The weather changes. Social mores change. The height of hemlines changes. Your task list changes. It's likely that some aspect of an item on your to-do list changed before you even finished entering the task in Outlook. Here, then, are two methods for modifying items on your task list.

Modifying a task the quick, simple way

You can easily change information about a task from the list where you view all your tasks. You can also change any information you see in any view (*see also* "Choosing a view" in Part V). It's this easy:

1. Click the item you want to change.

2. Select the old information by highlighting it.

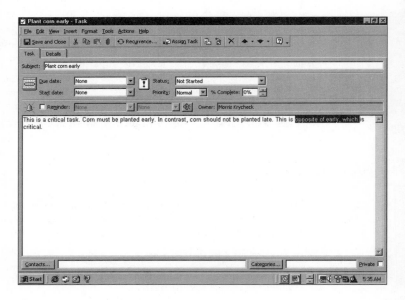

3. Type the new information.

4. Press the Enter key.

You can change any information you can see in any view of the Tasks module other than Timeline view. (For more general information about Outlook views, *see* "Choosing a view" in Part V.)

Modifying a task the slow, complete way

You can use the same method to change the information in a task that you used to enter the information in the first place. Although this slow, complete method requires a little more effort, you can enter much more precise information.

To modify a task slowly but completely, follow these steps:

1. If you're not already in the Tasks module, go to it by clicking the Tasks icon on the Outlook bar.

2. Choose View➪Current View➪Simple List.

3. To open the Task form, double-click the name of the task you want to change.

4. If you want to change the name of the task, click your mouse in the Subject text box and type a different name.

5. If you want to change the due date, click the Due Date box and enter the new due date.

6. If you want to change the start date, click the Start Date box and enter the new start date.

7. If you want to change the status of a task, click the scroll-down button at the right end of the Status box. A menu appears from which you can choose a different status.

8. If you want to choose a different priority level for a task, click the scroll-down button at the right end of the Priority box and choose your priority: low, medium, or high. If you leave the priority marking alone, your task will be marked as Normal.

9. If you want to turn the reminder on or off, click the Reminder check box.

10. If you want to enter or change the date when you want to be reminded, click the date box next to the Reminder check box; change the time you want to activate the reminder in the time box. Changing the reminder time is optional.

11. If you want to add or change miscellaneous notes and information about the task, click the text box at the bottom of the form and make whatever changes you want.

12. Click the Save and Close button (or press Alt+S) to finish.

I use the slow, complete way of changing task information only about 10 percent of the time because I'm too impatient to fill out a whole Task form. It's really not that much trouble, though.

Printing Tasks

Unless you have a photographic memory or one of the cool new pocket gizmos that store your task list, as well as your calendar, contacts, grocery list, and weather forecast, you may need to print one or more items on your task list. This section shows you how.

Printing a single task

After you've entered a task that includes lots of details about when, where, and how to do the task, you can print the task to give someone a copy or carry the copy around for your own reference.

Follow these steps to print a single task:

1. Click the name of the task to select it.

 2. Click the Print button on the toolbar to open the Print dialog box.

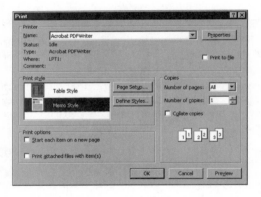

3. Choose Memo Style from the Print Style list.

4. If you want to print any document you may have attached to your task, click the box that says Print Attached Files with Item(s). (*See also* "Attaching a File to a Task Item," earlier in this part.)

5. Click OK.

Now you can run to the printer and wait for your printed output to appear in Beautiful, Living Black-and-White.

Printing a view

After you find a view that contains the information you want, printing that view is easy. You also can print the contents of each and every item.

To print a view, follow these steps:

1. Choose View⇨Current View and pick the view you want to print.

2. If you don't want to print every single item on the screen, select the ones you want to print by holding down the Ctrl key while clicking the tasks you want to print. The tasks you select are shaded blue to show that you've selected them. If you want to print all the items in the view, skip to the next step.

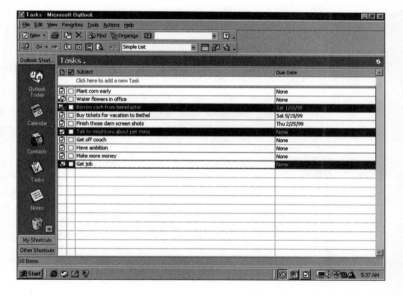

3. Click the Print button on the toolbar to open the Print dialog box.

4. Choose Table Style from the Print Style list. The other choice, Memo Style, prints each task as a full page in full detail.

5. If you want to print everything in the view, choose All Rows in the Print Range box. If you selected certain tasks in Step 2 and want to print only those, choose Only Selected Rows.

6. Click OK.

Remember that your printed output includes only items that appear in the view you chose before you clicked the Print button. What you see is what you get.

Sending a Task to Someone Else

The quickest way to get a task out of your hair is to get someone else to do it. Outlook enables you to send tasks to your coworkers for completion. However, your office network must be set up to allow it. If you're using Outlook on an office network that uses Microsoft Exchange Server, you can see status information entered by the person to whom you assigned the task. If your office network isn't set up to enable you to assign tasks (or if you're not on an office network), tasks you assign to others are received as e-mail messages.

To assign a task to someone else, follow these steps:

1. Double-click the task you want to assign to someone else.

2. Click the Assign Task button on the toolbar to open the Task form.

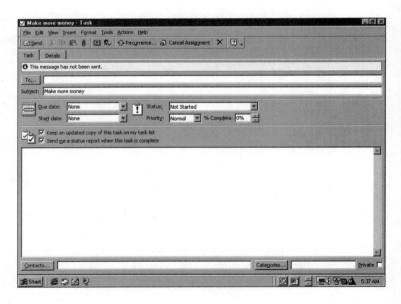

3. Type in the To box the name of the person to whom you want to assign the task. (This step presumes that you've already set up the person's name and e-mail address on your Contact list. If you haven't, *see* Part V.)

4. Click Send (or press Alt+S).

The task then appears on your Task list with a special icon next to it. The icon tells you that you've assigned this task to someone else for completion. If the task went out as an e-mail message, the message appears in your Sent Items folder (*see also* "Using the Sent Items folder," in Part II).

Assigning a task is the same as telling someone what to do. If the person to whom you're sending the task isn't required to do things at your request, some hard feelings could arise if you haven't cleared the request with that person first, so use discretion.

Setting the Color of Overdue or Completed Tasks

When a task becomes overdue, Outlook changes the color of the task name from the normal black to an alarming red to get your attention. Each task you've finished becomes gray with a line through it. If you prefer another way to display overdue and completed tasks, you can change it.

To change the color of overdue and completed tasks, follow these steps:

1. Choose Tools⇨Options to open the Options dialog box.

2. Click the Task Options button.

3. Click the scroll-down button at the right end of the Overdue Tasks box to see your choice of colors.

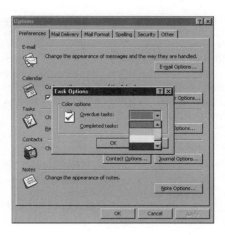

4. Choose a color for overdue tasks by clicking the color you want to use.

5. Click the scroll-down button at the right end of the Completed Tasks box to see your choice of colors.

6. Choose a color for completed tasks.

7. Click OK.

The Options dialog box disappears, and your tasks appear in Living Blue or Marvelous Magenta (or whatever you chose).

Skipping a Recurring Task Once

Now and then you may want to skip a task you've scheduled but still want to keep the other occurrences of that task set up.

To skip a recurring task, follow these steps:

1. Double-click the name of the task you want to skip. The Task form opens.

2. Choose Actions⇨Skip Occurrence.

3. Click the Save and Close button (or press Alt+S).

The due date of the task changes to the next scheduled due date for the task. Skipping one occurrence of a task leaves all the other occurrences unchanged.

Tracking the Progress of a Task

It's likely that your task list includes some entries for some longer, tougher projects. Perhaps you have some items like **build new house for mom** or **figure out way to get blood from a stone**. If your task list contain entries like these, you need a way to track your progress against completing these tasks because it's unlikely that you would complete 'em in one shot. At the same time, after a task is complete, you'll want to mark it accordingly so that so you can move on to your next task.

Marking a task as complete

Noting your accomplishments for the day is satisfying. You can do so by marking off each task as you add to the list of tasks you've finished, which you can also view. You can even send your boss a list of the tasks you've accomplished. First, however, you have to mark those tasks as complete (assuming that you've completed them).

To mark a task as complete, follow these steps:

1. If you're not in the Tasks module, switch to it by clicking the Tasks icon on the Outlook bar.

2. Choose View⇨Current View⇨Simple List.

3. Click the box next to the name of the task you want to mark as complete.

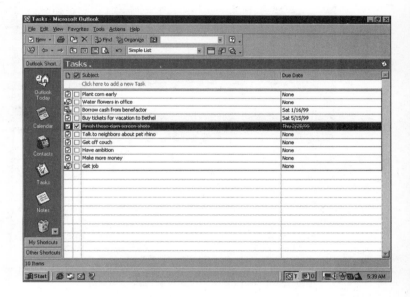

Outlook puts a line through the names of tasks you've completed if you're in Simple List view. If you're using a different view, such as Active Tasks view, your completed task vanishes entirely. To see only the tasks you've completed, use Completed Tasks view. For more information about views of your task list, *see* "Choosing a view," in Part V.

Marking several tasks as complete

Maybe you're too busy to sit around marking tasks as complete; maybe you wait until the end of the day to mark off your completed tasks in one fell swoop.

To mark several tasks as complete, follow these steps:

1. If you're not in the Tasks module, switch to it by clicking the Tasks icon on the Outlook bar.

2. Choose View⇨Current View⇨Simple List.

3. Click the first task you want to mark.

4. Hold down the Ctrl key and then click each of the other tasks you want to mark. The items you click turn blue to signify that you've selected them.

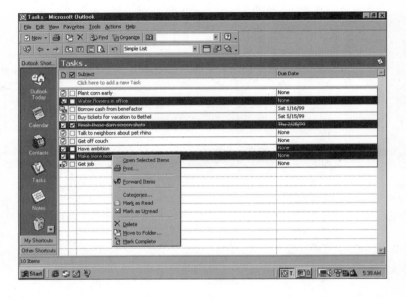

5. Right-click one of the tasks you've highlighted to display the shortcut menu.

6. Choose Mark Complete.

All the tasks you selected appear with a check mark to show that they're completed. A line appears through the name of the task to drive the point home.

Updating your progress on a task

As with a big meal, you may not be able to finish a task in one sitting. As with the remainder of the meal, you can, in effect, store the rest of the task in a doggie bag to finish later. To do so, all you do is enter the percentage complete for a task. The remainder of the task to be completed sort of resembles leftovers for your task list.

Follow these steps to update your progress:

1. If you're not already in the Tasks module, go to it by clicking the Tasks icon on the Outlook bar.

2. Choose <u>V</u>iew⇨Current <u>V</u>iew⇨Simple List.

3. To open the Task form, double-click the name of the task you want to change.

4. Choose the appropriate status for your task from the Status drop-down list: Not Started, In Progress, Completed, Waiting on Someone Else, Deferred.

5. If you want to enter a value for the amount of work you believe is complete on the task, click one of the arrow buttons beside the % Complete drop-down box to select a completion percent of either 0, 25%, 50%, or 75%. Click in the edit box to enter any value.

6. Click the Save and Close button (or press Alt+S).

Updating the hours worked on a task

You may want to track the total number of hours you needed to complete a task, especially one you couldn't complete in one sitting. In Outlook, you can keep track of the number of hours you have committed to a project.

Follow these steps to update your hours:

1. If you're not already in the Tasks module, go to it by clicking the Tasks icon on the Outlook bar.

2. Choose <u>V</u>iew⇨Current <u>V</u>iew⇨Simple List.

3. To open the Task form, double-click the name of the task you want to change.

4. Click the Status tab.

5. Update in the Actual Work field the number of hours you have worked on a task.

6. Click the Save and Close button (or press Alt+S).

Part V

Contacts

Outlook uses the word *Contacts* to mean people. I think that sounds sort of clandestine, but you may find it thrilling. Anyway, the Contact list is where you store people's names, addresses, phone numbers, and anything else you need to remember about the people in your life (maybe a code name?). You can collect a formidable dossier on each person in your Contact list, including a dozen different phone numbers and any kind of free-form information. You also can use the Find feature to quickly locate the information you've entered.

In this part . . .

- ✔ **Calling someone from Outlook**
- ✔ **Changing information about a contact**
- ✔ **Customizing the appearance of the Contact list**
- ✔ **Entering a new contact**
- ✔ **Finding a name, address, or phone number**
- ✔ **Printing a Contact list**

Calling Someone from Outlook

After you've entered the phone number for a contact, you don't have to settle for just looking up that person's number; you can make Outlook dial the number for you. You must have a modem attached to your computer and a phone attached to the modem, and, of course, you must already have the person's phone number entered on the Contact list.

To call someone from Outlook, follow these steps:

1. Click the Contacts icon on the Outlook bar. Your Contact list appears.

2. Click the name of the contact you want to call. The name is highlighted to show which name you chose.

3. Choose Actions⇨Call Contact and choose which of the contact's phone numbers you want to dial. The New Call dialog box appears.

4. If the number shown in the New Call dialog box is the number you want to dial, click Start Call. If the contact has more than one phone number, the first one that turns up in the New Call dialog box may not be the one you want, so click the scroll-down button next to the phone number and pick the number you want; then click Start Call to see the Call Status dialog box.

5. When the Call Status dialog box opens, pick up the phone.

6. When the person you're calling picks up the phone, click the Talk button in the Call Status dialog box to make the Call Status dialog box disappear.

7. After you finish the call, click the End Call button in the New Call dialog box. The phone hangs up when you click the End Call button.

8. Click the Close button to make the New Call dialog box disappear.

Changing Information about a Contact

The main advantage to saving names and addresses with a program like Outlook is that when the information you collect about the people you deal with changes over time, you can easily update your records.

Making changes to an item in your Contact list is simple. Just follow these steps:

1. Double-click the name of the contact you want to change. The contact item appears.

2. Click the information you want to change or click in the text box for the information you want to add. Type the new information.

3. Click the Save and Close button (or press Alt+S).

If you want to change information you added from Phone List view (*see also* "Adding a name the quick, simple way," later in this part), just click the information you want to change in Phone List view and enter the new information.

Customizing the Appearance of the Contact List

You can look at your Contact list in a variety of views, just as you can look at the information in all Outlook modules in a variety of ways. If you spend much time dealing with contacts, you can save a great deal of time by using the options for sorting, grouping, and filtering the different items in an Outlook view.

About views

Although Outlook comes with dozens of different views and you can create hundreds more if you want, it has only a handful of basic view types. You can see what the choices are by choosing View⇨Current View⇨Define Views and then clicking the New button. (After you've finished looking, press Esc twice to return to the screen where you started.)

If this list seems small, think of each type of view as though it were a type of recipe. Five types of recipes — appetizers, salads, soups, entrées, and desserts — can be the basis for an unlimited number of recipes. You can cook up an equally endless variety of views, beginning with these five general types. The Create a New View dialog box enables you to choose from among only five basic types of views in any Outlook module:

✦ **Table:** Your plain-vanilla arrangement of rows and columns. Phone List view in the Contacts module, Simple List view in the Tasks module, and Active Appointments view in the Calendar are all examples of table-type views.

✦ **Timeline:** Draws a picture depicting each item in a view, either in order of their due dates or the date when you dealt with them. The Inbox, Tasks, and Journal modules all include Timeline views. No real need exists for a Timeline view of your Contact list, although you can create one (*see also* "Saving and deleting created views," later in this part).

✦ **Card:** Looks like a collection of file cards. Address Cards view and Detailed Address Cards view in your Contacts module are the only examples of card views included with Outlook.

✦ **Day/Week/Month:** Calendar-style views designed for — you guessed it — the Calendar module.

✦ **Icons:** Fill the screen with icons representing each item and a title that matches the title of the item. The Notes module uses Icons view.

Choosing a view

Contact views come with Outlook when you first start the program. These views cover things for which most people use the Contact list. You can add as many views as you need, however, so don't feel limited by the initial selection. Here's what you have when you begin:

✦ **Address Cards:** Looks like a screen full of little file cards arranged in alphabetical order. You see only a few key items in Address Cards view, such as name, mailing address, phone number, and e-mail address.

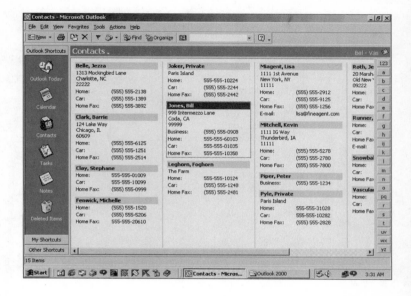

✦ **Detailed Address Cards:** A more detailed version of Address Cards view. This view shows everything on the first page of the Contact form, including the person's title, company, and the first few lines of text from the text box at the bottom of the Contact form.

✦ **Phone List:** Turns your collection of contacts into a plain-looking list of names, addresses, and phone numbers. Phone List view is not as pretty as Address Cards view or Detailed Address Cards view. However, you can sort, group, and categorize your contacts in this view in ways that aren't possible in those other two views.

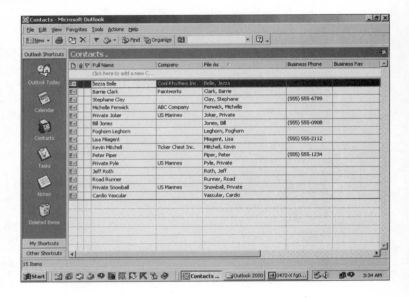

+ **By Category:** Looks similar to Phone List view, but does a trick called *grouping*. Contacts are clumped together according to the category you've assigned to each of them. Contacts not assigned a category are clumped into a category called None.

+ **By Company:** Similar to By Category view: They are both grouped views (grouped views in Outlook usually have a name that starts with the word *By*). This view groups items according to the company you've entered for each contact.

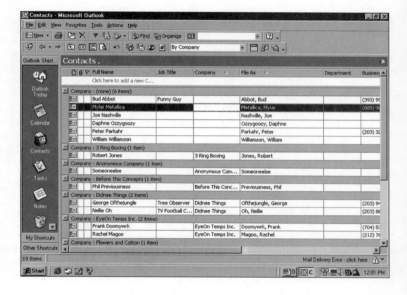

✦ **By Location:** Like the other two By views. This view gathers contacts together — in this case, according to the country you've entered for each contact. I changed my By Location view to group by state because I have few contacts outside the United States. If you have contacts in many countries, however, you can leave the location setup alone.

✦ **By Follow-Up Flag:** Shows a list of your messages according to which kind of flag you assigned to each message.

See also "Saving and deleting created views," later in this part, to find out how to change a view to suit your needs and save it.

Switching between views in any Outlook module is as simple as changing channels on your TV. Choose View➪Current View and then pick the view you want. If you don't like the new view, just switch back by using the same commands to choose the view you were looking at before.

Filtering Views

Filtered views show only items that have certain characteristics, such as a certain job title or a certain date. All views in all Outlook modules can be filtered, and some modules include filtered views. The Calendar module includes an Events view, which shows only items that are classified as events (*see also* "Reviewing Your Calendar" in Part III). The Tasks module has a view called Next Seven Days, which filters out all tasks except those whose due date falls within the next seven days (*see also* "Choosing a view," earlier in this part). When you're using a filtered view, the words *Filter Applied* appear on the folder banner, just above the information viewer.

Although the Contacts module doesn't come with any filtered views when you begin using Outlook, you can easily create filtered views of your Contact list. Filtered views are useful if you frequently need to see a list of contacts who work at different companies but have the same job title, such as president or sales manager. You may also want to create a filtered view of contacts who live in your immediate vicinity if you need to call on customers in person. Use this process for filtering a view and then save the view (*see also* "Saving and deleting created views," later in this part).

To filter items in a view, follow these steps:

1. Choose View➪Current View➪Customize Current View to open the View Summary dialog box.

2. Click the Filter button to open the Filter dialog box.

3. Enter the text you want to filter in the box labeled Search for the Word(s). For example, if you want to see only the names of people whose job title is president, type the word *president* in the box.

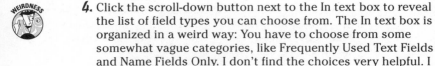

4. Click the scroll-down button next to the In text box to reveal the list of field types you can choose from. The In text box is organized in a weird way: You have to choose from some somewhat vague categories, like Frequently Used Text Fields and Name Fields Only. I don't find the choices very helpful. I have managed to find what I'm looking for most often when I choose Frequently Used Text Fields.

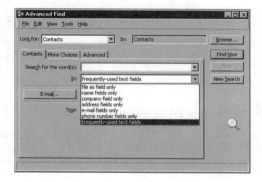

5. Click OK to filter your list. The words *Filter Applied* appear on the folder banner, and your list shows only the items that match the text you entered in Step 3.

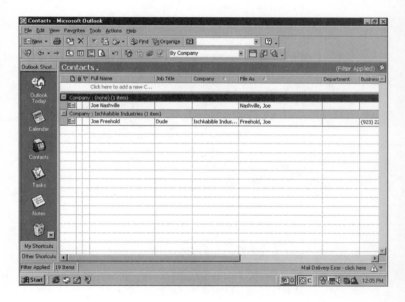

The reason the words *Filter Applied* appear is to let you know that the view you're seeing shows only items that match some kind of filter. That's important to know because you still can create new items while looking at a filtered view. If you create a new item that doesn't match the filter while looking at a filtered view, the item you create seems to disappear. For example, if you're using a filtered view that shows only the names of presidents of companies and you create a contact for someone whose job title is sales manager, that contact doesn't appear on a list filtered to show only presidents. To see sales managers, you have to switch to a view that shows everybody on the list, not just presidents.

Putting new fields in a view

Most Outlook views display fewer than a dozen fields, even though items in nearly every Outlook module can store several dozen fields. You can even create your own fields. You can add fields to any Outlook view and use the fields you add to sort, group, or filter your collection of items.

To add a field to any Outlook view, follow these steps:

1. Choose <u>V</u>iew⇨Current <u>V</u>iew⇨Customize Current View to open the View Summary dialog box.

2. Click the Fields button. The Show Fields dialog box opens.

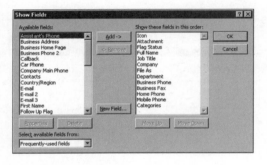

3. Click the name of the field you want to add in the Available Fields list box. The name you click is highlighted to show which field you chose.

4. Click Add. The field you chose is copied to the bottom of the Show These Fields in This Order box.

5. Click Move Up to move the field you chose higher on your list. Every time you click Move Up, your field moves up one position on the list. The highest items on the list are displayed closest to the top of any Address Cards view and leftmost in any Table view.

6. Click OK to close the Show Fields dialog box. Your new field is displayed in the position you selected.

If the field you want to add doesn't appear on the Available Fields list, you may need to choose a different collection of fields from the box labeled Select Available Fields From. Although the default choice is Frequently Used Fields, you find more choices if you pick a choice that begins with the word *All,* such as All Contact Fields or All Task Fields. When you do, a much larger selection of fields appears.

Rearranging views

List-type views, such as Phone List view, can have more columns of information than fit on the screen. Sometimes, placing two columns together makes them easier to use, such as when you place the name and phone number columns together.

To move the phone number next to the person's name, follow these steps:

1. Choose View➪Current View➪Phone List to see your phone list.

2. Click the Business Phone heading and drag it on top of the Full Name column. The gray heading box containing the words *Business Phone* moves where you drag it.

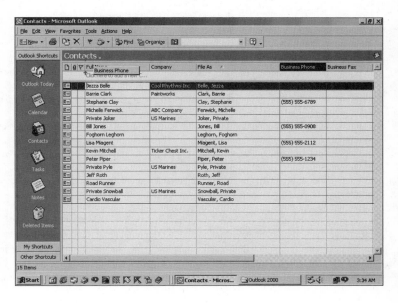

3. Release the mouse button.

As you drag the heading across the screen, you see two red arrows moving along the row of remaining column headings. When you release the mouse button, the heading you dragged (in this case, the Business Phone heading) drops into the row of headings specifically in the spot where the arrows point.

Saving and deleting created views

You can save any view you create and use it over and over. To create and save a view, follow these steps:

1. Create a custom view by dragging any column heading to a new location or to the Group By box. Your list appears as a grouped view.

2. Choose <u>V</u>iew⇨Current <u>V</u>iew⇨Define Views to open the Define Views dialog box.

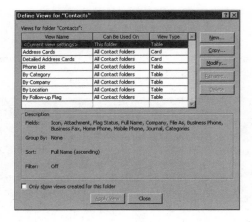

3. Click Copy to open the Copy View dialog box.

4. Type under Name of New View (what else?) the name you want to give your new view.

5. Click OK to close the Copy View dialog box. (Leave the rest of the settings alone for now.) The name you gave to your new view now appears on the list of views for this folder.

6. Click Close to close the Define Views dialog box.

The name of any view you create and save appears on the Current View menu. You can use the view you create at any time, just like you use any other view.

If you change your mind or just don't need to use that view anymore, you can easily delete any view you created and saved.

To delete a created view, follow these steps:

1. Choose View➪Current View➪Define Views. The Define Views dialog box appears.

2. Click the name of the view you want to delete and then click the Delete button. A dialog box appears, asking whether you're sure.

3. If you're sure, click OK.

4. Click Close.

The Delete button appears only when you click the name of a view you created. If you try to delete a view that's built in to Outlook, such as Phone List view, the Delete button doesn't appear, preventing you from accidentally deleting something you shouldn't.

Sorting a view the quick, simple way

Certain views of your Contact list are more useful when you organize the items according to a single piece of information, such as the contact's last name, company affiliation, city, or state.

You can quickly sort some views, such as Phone List view, by clicking the heading of any column you want to sort. For example, you can sort your phone list according to the company for which each person on your Contact list works.

To sort your phone list by the contact's company, follow these steps:

1. Choose View➪Current View➪Phone List to show your phone list.

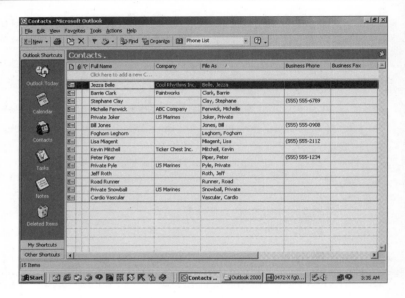

2. Click the heading of the Company column to reorder the whole list according to the name of each contact's company.

You can sort any list by clicking any column heading, except Category, in an Outlook view. Remember, though, that you can use only the quick, simple method to sort a view that looks like a list (a Table view, in Outlook-speak). Other views, such as Address Cards views, don't have column headings you can click to make the list sort itself. In those cases, you have to use the slow, complete way to sort, which is next.

Sorting a view the slow, complete way

The quick, simple method of sorting your views works only in list views. Views such as Address Cards view require a different method of sorting that takes more time. Nor does the quick, simple method work when you're sorting a list by a piece of information not showing on the list. For example, because the phone list normally doesn't show the state in which each contact lives, you can't do a quick sort of the phone list by state.

Each piece of information you enter about a contact is called a *field*. Each field shows up as a separate column in Phone List view. However, each field shows up as a separate *line* in Address Cards view. When you use the slow, complete method of sorting your

Contact list (or sorting the items in any Outlook module), the Sort dialog box refers to each item as a field (Name field or State field, for example).

The slow, complete method takes a little more time but gives you more choices.

To sort a view according to each contact's state, follow these steps:

1. Choose View➪Current View➪Edit Current View to open the View Summary dialog box.

2. Click the Sort button to open the Sort dialog box.

3. Click the scroll-down menu under Sort Items By and choose State from the menu. The word *State* appears in the Sort Items By box.

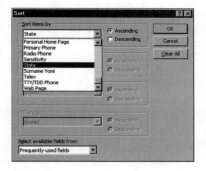

4. Click Ascending if you want your view to begin with contacts from states that begin with the letter *A,* like Alabama and Alaska. Click Descending if you want your view organized in reverse alphabetical order, starting with Wyoming and West Virginia. A black spot appears in the circle next to whichever choice you click.

5. Click OK to begin sorting your list.

6. Choose Yes if a dialog box appears saying that the field "state" you want to sort by is not shown in the view and asking whether you want to show it. (Frankly, whether you choose Yes or No in this dialog box doesn't matter much; however, don't pick Cancel or else Outlook doesn't sort the list.)

Sometimes you still can't see the field you added, even after you click Yes to the question about showing the field. In views such as Phone List, Outlook adds the new field at the far right end of the list, so you have to scroll way over to see it. If you want to re-arrange the list so that you easily can see the newly added field, see "Rearranging views," earlier in this part.

When you open the Sort dialog box, you see four nearly identical boxes. These boxes enable you to choose as many as four fields when you're sorting your view. Outlook sorts the view according to which fields you choose in the order in which you choose them.

Using grouped views

The names of many Outlook views begin with the word *By,* which means that they are grouped views. The Contacts module has four built-in grouped views: By Category, By Company, By Follow-Up Flag, and By Location, although you can create any custom groupings you need. A *grouped* view clumps the items in the view into groups that have the same piece of information in a certain field. For example, the By Company field clumps together all the contacts from each company. The following figure shows your contacts grouped by company; the one after that shows contacts grouped by country and region.

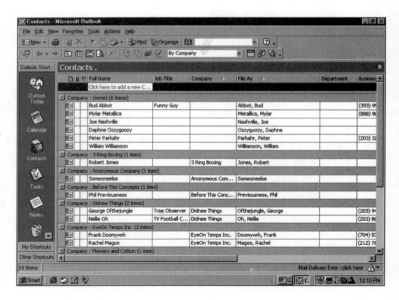

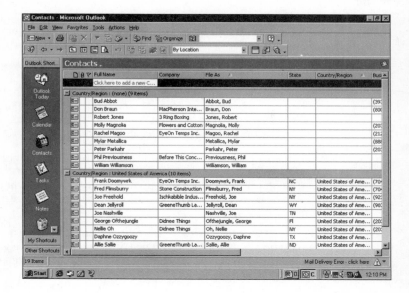

Each group in a grouped view is represented by a gray bar that has a plus or minus sign on the left side. A plus-sign icon tells you that you have more to see in the group. Just click the plus sign to open the group and see which contacts belong to that group. A minus sign means that the total group is open; you're seeing all there is to see.

Using your own groups with the Group By box

If the grouped views that come with Outlook aren't enough for you, you can always create your own grouped views by using the Group By box.

To create your own grouped views, follow these steps:

1. Choose View➪Toolbars➪Advanced to display the Advanced toolbar. You may want to leave it displayed all the time to take advantage of its wider selection of tools. Some folks become confused when faced with too many tools, so they leave the Advanced toolbar hidden most of the time.

2. Click the Group By box button on the Advanced toolbar to open the Group By box. The Group By box appears just above the column headings and says Drag a Column Header Here to Group By That Column.

3. Drag a column header to the gray box to group by that column. (You probably figured that out without my help.) The list now appears as a grouped view, with each group of items separated by a gray bar that describes the group (*see also* "Using grouped views," earlier in this part).

If you change your mind and want to group by a different column, simply drag the header back to the header row you got it from and then drag another header up to the Group By box. You can even drag two or more headers up to the Group By box to create groups within groups.

Warning: The order in which you add multiple headers to the Group By box makes a big difference in how the items are grouped. If you decide to group by city and state, for example, it makes more sense to group by state first and then by city because states contain cities, so your State groups automatically should contain City groups. Confused? Just give it a try. Anything you can drag into the Group By box can be dragged back to where it came from, so you can't do any harm.

Entering a New Contact

In the Contacts module, you can save and organize nearly any type of information about the people you deal with. You then can find everything again lickety-split. If you want, you can enter quick scraps of information without interrupting the flow of your work. You also can spend the time to enter minutely detailed information every time you create a new contact.

Adding a name the quick, simple way

The quick, simple way of entering names on your Contact list may be too limited: You simply can't enter all the information you may need. At times, however, you need to save only a person's name, company, and phone number, so having a quick way to save this information is a good thing.

To enter names on your Contact list, follow these steps:

1. If you're not in the Contacts module, click the Contacts icon on the Outlook bar.

2. Choose View⇨Current View⇨Phone List to reveal a simple list of names and addresses.

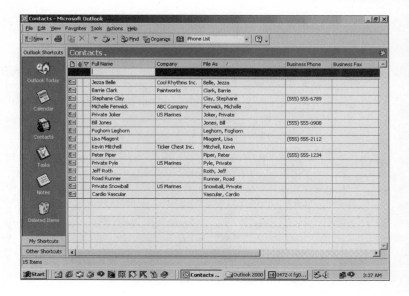

3. Click the first line of the phone list. A message appears that says *Click here to enter a new contact.* (Don't be alarmed if the message says only *Click here to enter a n.* That's just what Outlook does when the column is too narrow. Just click anyway.) You can change the width of any column in any Outlook view by dragging the right border at the top of the column in the header row (*see also* "Get the best fit" in Part VIII).

4. Type the name of the person you want to enter on your Contact list.

5. Press Tab to move to the next column, labeled Company. Type the name of the company for which the person works.

6. Keep pressing Tab to move right one column at a time, and enter whatever information you want, including phone numbers, fax numbers, and categories.

7. After you're finished, press Enter to make your new contact drop down into the list with your other contacts.

If you want to enter more information, you can always reopen the item and change anything you want at another time. I find it quicker to get a name and phone number and then add the other stuff later.

Adding a name the slow, complete way

Adding names to your Contact list is as simple as filling out a form. You don't have to fill in everything the form asks for — just the name of the contact you're entering. While you're entering the name, you may as well enter other things you need to know about the person, such as an address, phone number, e-mail address, Web page address, and whatever.

To add a name to your Contact list, follow these steps:

1. Click the Contacts icon on the Outlook bar, if you're not already in the Contacts module.

2. Click the New Contact button on the toolbar. The New Contact form appears.

3. Enter the person's name in the Full Name box. When you open the New Contact Form, the insertion point is already in the Full Name text box, so you don't have to click anywhere. Enter the first name and then the last name, such as **George Washington**.

Outlook automatically figures which is the first name and which is the last name, and it makes sense of prefixes and suffixes like Dr., Mr., and Jr. If you plan to use your Contact list to create form letters in Microsoft Word, click the Full Name button to see how Outlook dealt with the name. Outlook gets it right more often than not, but if you see the first name in the Middle name box or the last name in the Suffix box, you can enter the correct names in the proper boxes.

Whenever you enter a name, such as **George Washington**, in the Full Name text box and then press Tab or click your mouse in any other box, the name appears again in the File As box — except that now the name appears last name first: Washington, George. The entry in the File As box tells you how Outlook plans to file your contact — in this case, by the last name, in the W section. You also can file a contact according to some other word. For example, George Washington could also be filed under F, for father of our country. More practical examples are filing the name of your plumber under the word *plumber,* your auto mechanic under *mechanic,* and so on.

4. Click the Address box and enter the person's address. Outlook interprets addresses by using the same method it uses to make sense of names. Breaking the address into street, city, state, zip code, and country enables you to use the Outlook Contact list as a source of addresses when you're creating form letters in Microsoft Word. You don't have to do anything to make Outlook perform this interpretation trick (*parsing,* as the techies call it), but you may want to double-check the Outlook interpretation by clicking the Address button. After you click it, the Check Address dialog box appears, showing you how Outlook interpreted the address you entered. If the name of the city wound up in the State/Province box or the name of the state wound up in the Zip/Postal Code box, you can fix everything in the Check Address dialog box.

5. Click the check box labeled This Is the Mailing Address if the address you've just entered is the contact address to which you plan to send mail.

6. Click in the text box to the right of the Business Phone box and type the contact's business phone number.

7. Click in the text box to the right of the Home Phone box and type the contact's home phone number.

8. Click in the text box to the right of the E-Mail Address list box and enter your contact's e-mail address.

9. Click in the Web Page text box if the contact has a Web page. Enter the *Uniform Resource Locator (URL),* or Web address, for that page so that you can link to that page directly from the address card.

10. Click in the large text box at the bottom of the form and type anything you want.

11. Click the Categories button in the bottom-left corner of the screen to assign a category to the contact, if you want.

12. Click the name of each category that applies to your contact. If none of the existing categories suits you, click Master Category List in the lower-right corner to see the Master Category list box.

13. Type the name of a new category in the Item(s) Belong to These Categories box at the top of the Master Category list box.

14. Click Add and then click OK to return to the Categories list.

15. Click the name of the category you've just added, which now appears on the Categories list.

16. Click OK to close the Categories list and return to the New Contact form.

17. Click the Private box in the lower-right corner of the Contact form if you're on a network and don't want others to know about your contacts. After you click the Private box, you should see a check mark to indicate that it's turned on.

18. Click the Journal tab in the top-left corner of the form to set your journaling preferences. The Journal page appears.

19. After you're finished, click the Save and Close button (or press Alt+S) to close the New Contact form.

With the help of Outlook, you can easily save and recall a huge list of items about all your contacts. Do as much or little as you want. You always can go back and make changes later.

Finding a Name, Address, or Phone Number

I assume that you want to find the names of your contacts sometime in the future, if you take the time to enter them in the first place. The quick, simple way to find a contact is simply to look up the name. Sometimes, however, you can't remember the name. You may recall something else about the person that you know you entered — such as the company she works for or the city where he lives. This section shows you several ways you can dig up information about your contacts.

Finding a contact the quick, simple way

The quick, simple way of finding a contact assumes that you remember the last name or the word you used in the File As box.

To find a contact by last name, follow these steps:

1. Choose <u>V</u>iew⇨Current <u>V</u>iew⇨Address Cards (for more information about choosing views, see "Choosing a view," earlier in this part). Address Cards view looks like a deck of address cards laid out across your screen.

2. Type the first letter of the contact's last name. The view moves to the part of Address Cards view that contains people whose names begin with that letter.

3. If you still don't see the person's name, press the right-arrow key to scroll through the list alphabetically.

If you entered something other than the contact's name in the File As box, such as *plumber* or *dentist,* press the letter *p* for plumber or *d* for dentist (*see also* "Adding a name the slow, complete way," earlier in this part).

Finding a contact by using the Advanced Find feature

You can use the Find button on the toolbar to find a contact quickly the same way you find any other Outlook item (*see also* "Finding a Note" in Part VII), although the Advanced Find feature can do a more detailed search, if that's what you want. Sometimes you can't recall the name of the person you're looking for but you remember some fragment of the information you entered about his. For example, you remember that his name ends with *Jr* or you remember that he lives in Omaha. The Find Items feature finds all items that contain the tiniest scrap of information you entered.

To search for a contact by using Advanced Find, follow these steps:

1. Choose Tools➪Advanced Find (or press Ctrl+Shift+F) to open the Advanced Find dialog box.

2. Click the scroll-down button at the right end of the Look For text box.

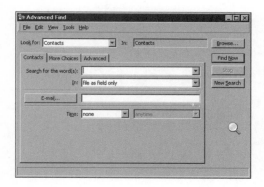

3. Choose Contacts from the menu. If you start from the Contacts module, the Look For box should already say *Contacts.*

4. Click the triangle at the right end of the In text box on the Contacts tab to see the list of parts of the Contact list you can search.

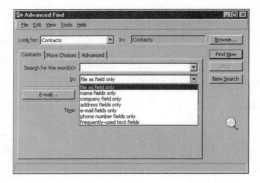

5. Choose Frequently-Used Text Fields.

6. Click the Search for the Word(s) text box and enter the text you want to find.

7. Click the Find Now button. A little magnifying glass turns in circles while Outlook finds contact items that contain the text you entered. When items are found, their names appear on a list at the bottom of the Advanced Find dialog box.

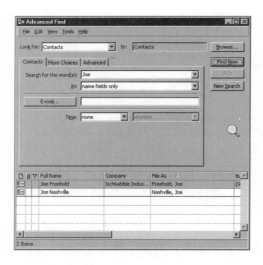

8. Double-click the name of a contact on the list at the bottom of the Find Items dialog box to see that person's Contact record.

After you open a Contact record located by the Find Items feature, the Find Items dialog box remains open in the background, in case you want to open another contact that turned up in your search. Just click the icon on the Windows taskbar at the bottom of the

Contact Record screen that says Find – Contacts to return to the Find Items dialog box. Press Esc to close the Find Items dialog box after you're finished.

Printing Contact Lists

You can print your Contact lists in a variety of styles. The two basic types of views available on the Contact list — Address Cards and Table — each appear in their own style when you print them.

Printing Address Cards views

When you're viewing the Contacts module from Address Cards view or Detailed Address Cards view, you can choose from several print styles. These styles organize the contact information you print in the same way it's organized on the screen, as a series of boxes, each containing information about one contact.

To print address cards, follow these steps:

1. Choose View⇨Current View⇨Address Cards to switch to that view.

2. Click the Print button on the toolbar (or press Ctrl+P) to open the Print dialog box.

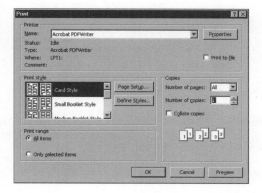

3. Choose the style you want from the Print Style list:

Card: Prints your contacts in a style that looks much like the address cards you see on the screen.

Small Booklet: Prints your Contact list in Address Cards view but arranges the cards in a way that enables you to cut up the pages and staple them together to form a pocket-size address directory.

Medium Booklet: Just like Small Booklet Style except that it creates a larger booklet.

Memo: Prints only contacts you've selected by clicking with your mouse before clicking the Print button. All the information you've entered about the contact appears in a style that looks like a business memorandum.

Phone Directory: Prints in alphabetical order only the names and phone numbers of your contacts.

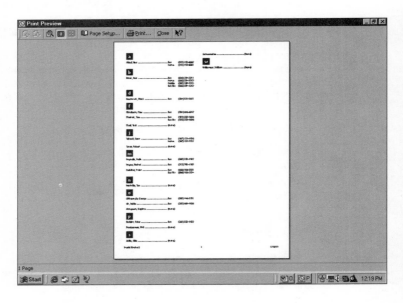

4. Click OK to send your list to the printer.

If you want to select more than one contact in order to print multiple contacts in Memo Style, hold down the Ctrl key while clicking each contact you want to include.

Printing from Table views

Printing lists of your contacts from Table-style views, such as in Phone List view or By Company view, enables you to take advantage of the grouping and sorting tricks you can do in Outlook views.

When you print from a Table view, remember: WYSIWYG! What you see is what you get. If you click the Print button while viewing the By Category view, the By Category view is what you print.

To print from a Table view, follow these steps:

1. Choose a Table-style view, such as Phone List or By Company.

 2. Click the Print button on the toolbar (or press Ctrl+P) to open the Print dialog box.

3. Choose the style you want from the Print Style list:

Table: Prints exactly what you see on the screen.

Memo: Prints only contacts you've selected by clicking with your mouse before clicking the Print button. All the information you've entered about the contact appears in a style that looks like a business memorandum.

Phone Directory: Prints in alphabetical order only the names and addresses of your contacts.

4. Click OK to start printing your list.

 You do the same things to print from Outlook as you do to print from any Windows program: Just put what you want to print on the screen and then click the Print button.

Part VI

Journal

The Journal can do most of its work for you invisibly. After you set up Outlook to make journal entries of your documents, tasks, and contacts, you use the Journal only when you want to look at the things it recorded. It keeps a record of the things you've done.

The Journal is the one part of Outlook that can be useful even if you never look at it. If you don't mess with the Journal other than to turn the feature on, you still have a record of every document you create and every e-mail message you send and receive and a chronology of most of your important interactions with the people on your Contact list.

If you *do* use your Journal, you can keep track of meetings, phone calls, conversations, and a number of other routine events. Why would you want all this information? Because sometimes it's hard to remember what you named a document you created or the folder in which you saved a certain spreadsheet. But you *may* remember when you did what you did — like last Thursday.

In this part . . .

✔ **Activating the automatic recording feature**

✔ **Creating Journal entries manually with drag-and-drop**

✔ **Creating Journal entries with the New Journal Item button**

✔ **Finding Journal entries and printing them**

✔ **Seeing Journal entries for a Contact**

✔ **Viewing the Journal or a specific date in your Journal**

Activating the Automatic Recording Feature

You wouldn't really be lying if you said that you don't have to do anything to make the Journal work for you. You would be exaggerating a little, though. Although you do have to tell the Journal to record everything, you have to tell it only once.

To activate the Journal's automatic recording feature, follow these steps:

1. Choose Tools⇨Options. The Options dialog box opens.

2. Click the Journal Options button to open the Journal Options dialog box.

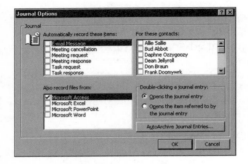

3. Click to place a check in the check box for the items and files you want to record automatically and for the contacts about whom you want the information recorded.

4. Click OK.

One peculiarity about the Journal is that you can't blithely check off a box that says "Record everything about all my contacts." You must check off every contact's name in the Journal Options dialog box. Alternatively, you can check the Automatically Record Journal Entries for This Contact check box on the Journal tab. This box is on the Contact form when you create each new contact entry. In my humble opinion, this arrangement is silly, but for the moment, you're stuck with it.

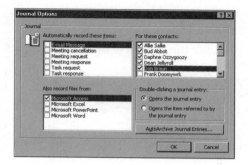

Creating Journal Entries Manually with Drag-and-Drop

Even though the Cold War is over, you may be skittish about having some computer record all your activities. (I think that James Bond would have loved the Journal.) On the other hand, it's nice to have a record of important things, like phone calls, without exerting too much effort. You can use the manual (drag-and-drop) method to record individual events in your Journal.

To record individual events by using the drag-and-drop method, follow these steps:

1. Drag to the Journal icon the item you want to record (such as an e-mail message). A new Journal Entry form opens.

2. Fill in any information you want to record.

3. Click Save and Close (or press Alt+S).

Your e-mail message (or whatever you dragged to the Journal icon) is now immortalized in your Journal. Congratulations!

Creating Journal Entries with the New Journal Item Button

Drag-and-drop isn't the only method of creating new Journal entries. You can make a new Journal entry for any reason at all. Simply go to the Journal and create a new item.

To create a new Journal entry, follow these steps:

1. Click the Journal icon on the Outlook bar, if you're not in the Journal module.

New ▾

2. Click the New Journal item button on the toolbar. The Journal Entry form opens.

3. Enter the subject of the Journal entry in the Subject text box.

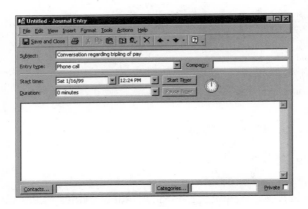

4. Click the scroll-down button in the Entry Type box to pick an entry type.

5. If you want to add any other information to the Journal entry, enter it in the appropriate text box.

6. Click <u>S</u>ave and Close (or press Alt+S). Your new Journal entry now appears in your Journal.

You can't easily add Journal entry types the way you can add new categories (but you can assign categories to Journal entries). If you are frequently served with legal papers, for example, you may want to make an entry type called Documents Served or something similar. That's fairly difficult to do, however. (Okay, you *can* edit the Windows Registry to add Journal entry types, but — hoo-boy! — I wouldn't recommend getting into that!) You can just make a Journal entry for a letter and put it in a category of your choice, the same way you would for any Outlook item (***see also*** "Assigning a Category to a Note" in Part VII).

Finding a Journal Entry

Although the Journal is time-oriented (it tracks items by time and date), occasionally you may need to find a Journal entry without knowing when the entry was made. To dig up the Journal entry you want, simply use the Find Items button.

To find a Journal entry, follow these steps:

1. Click the Journal icon on the Outlook bar. Your list of Journal entries appears.

2. Click the Find button on the toolbar (or press Alt+I). The Find window opens.

3. Enter in the Look For text box a word or phrase you can find in your Journal.

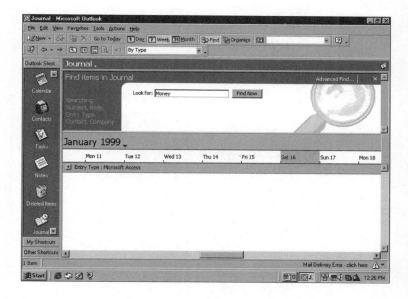

4. If the Journal entry you're looking for turns up, double-click the icon next to the entry to see the item's contents. If the entry you're looking for doesn't show up, try searching for different text.

5. Click the Find button again (or press Alt+I) to close the Find window.

The icon that appears in the text box of your Journal entry is a shortcut to the document. You can open the document by double-clicking the shortcut.

Printing Journal Entries

If you're like me, you just don't get the same picture from a screen that you do from a good ol' piece of paper. It's a good thing you can print your Journal entries.

To print entries from your Journal, follow these steps:

1. Click the Journal icon on the Outlook bar. Your list of Journal entries appears.

2. Choose from the Current View menu the view in which you want to print.

3. Select the entries you want to print (unless you want to print them all).

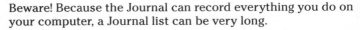

   Beware! Because the Journal can record everything you do on your computer, a Journal list can be very long.

4. Click the Print button on the toolbar (or press Ctrl+P). The Print dialog box opens.

5. Choose Table or Memo format.

6. Choose All Rows or Only Selected Rows.

7. Click OK to print your Journal entries.

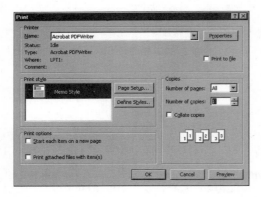

The Print dialog box has a Preview button, which enables you to see what you're about to print before you commit everything to paper. Because a Journal can quickly develop thousands of entries, you would do well to preview what you print before tying up your printer with a document that could be more than a hundred pages long. Your office mates will thank you.

Seeing Journal Entries for a Contact

Automatic journaling of your interactions with your contacts is one benefit you can get from the Journal.

To see what you gained from the Journal, follow these steps:

1. Click the Contacts icon on the Outlook bar. The Contact list appears.

2. Double-click the name of the contact you want to view. The Contact form opens.

3. Click the drop-down arrow at the end of the Show box on the Contact form to see Journal entries for that contact.

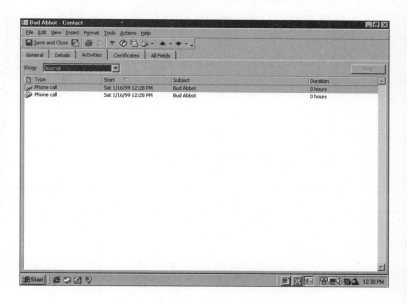

Remember, though, that you have to check Automatically Record Journal Entries for This Contact in order to create the automatic entries you see on this page. Another way to generate journal entries is to use the AutoDial feature on the Contact list and check the box that says Create New Journal Entry When Starting New Call.

Viewing the Journal

You can view your Journal entries in a variety of screen arrangements, called *views*. When you first start Outlook, six views are already set up for you to use with the Journal. You can switch among them by choosing View⇨Current View and picking the name of the view you want. If one view doesn't suit you, switch to another view in the same way.

This list describes each of those six built-in views:

+ **By Type:** Groups your Journal entries on a timeline according to the type of entry, such as e-mail messages, Excel spreadsheets, or Word documents. You can scroll forward and back in time to see different slices of your Journal.

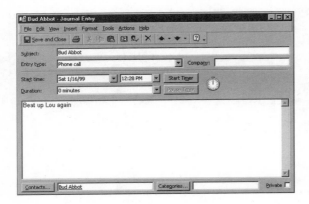

+ **By Contact:** Another grouped timeline view that organizes your Journal entries according to the contact associated with each entry. You cannot print the By Contact view of the Journal.

+ **By Category:** Looks much like the By Type view except that the entries are grouped according to the category you've assigned each entry. You cannot print the By Category view of the Journal.

+ **Entry List:** A simple list of all your Journal entries. You can sort the Entry List according to any piece of information listed, such as subject, contact, starting time, or duration. You also can select and copy a range of entries from the Entry List. You then can paste the range into an Excel spreadsheet to calculate the total time spent on work for a certain contact or on projects in a certain category.

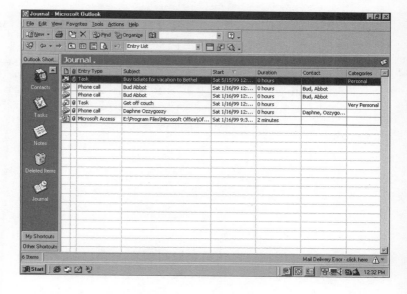

+ **Last Seven Days:** Just like the Entry List except that it hides entries that occurred more than seven days ago.

+ **Phone Calls:** Shows only the phone calls you've entered in your Journal.

Viewing a Specific Date in Your Journal

If you use the Journal to record your activities, you accumulate lots of information. Sometimes the amount of information is so great that sorting through all the entries becomes difficult.

To see only the activities on a certain date, follow these steps:

1. Click the Journal icon on the Outlook bar. The Journal appears.

2. Choose any view that begins with the word *By* (By Type, By Contact, or By Category) by choosing <u>V</u>iew⇨Current <u>V</u>iew and picking the view you want.

3. Choose <u>G</u>o⇨Go to Dat<u>e</u> (or press Ctrl+G). The Go To Date dialog box opens.

4. In the Date box, enter the date you want to view, such as **December 16, 1998,** or type the amount of time since the date you have in mind, such as **two weeks ago**.

The display shifts to the date you asked for, and you see a collection of icons representing the Journal entries for the date you specified. If no entries exist, no icons appear.

Part VII

Notes

Nothing is easier to use than those yellow sticky notes, which is probably why you see them everywhere. I like to stick those little yellow scraps of paper just about anywhere. But, quick as a wink, I forget where I stuck them. Outlook notes are just as easy to use, and they're much easier to find.

The Notes module enables you to keep quick, bite-size nuggets of information that are too important to forget but not important enough to open your word processor to write home about.

In this part . . .

- ✓ Assigning a category to a note
- ✓ Changing the color and size of a note
- ✓ Creating, using, and viewing notes
- ✓ Deleting a note
- ✓ Finding a note
- ✓ Forwarding a note to someone else
- ✓ Printing a list of notes and the contents of a single note
- ✓ Setting note default options
- ✓ Turning off the date-and-time display
- ✓ Viewing notes

Assigning a Category to a Note

You can assign a category to any note you create in Outlook. Categories may be a little more useful when you're using the Notes module than when you're using other parts of Outlook, because you can enter any ol' kind of information in a note, which can make it hard to find later. Assigning categories makes the stuff you collect easier to use and understand.

To assign a category to a note, follow these steps:

1. Click the Note icon in the upper-left corner of the note. The shortcut menu appears.

2. Choose Categories. The Categories dialog box appears.

3. Choose one of the existing categories, if one suits you; then click OK.

4. If none of the existing categories suits you, enter a category of your choice in the New Category box.

5. Click OK. Although your note looks the same, now it has a category.

I prefer to choose categories from the Category list rather than type my own because using the listed categories keeps your organization consistent and the list easy to use. For example, I never remember whether I called the category I created *References* or just named it *Refs*. Although I mean the same thing in both cases, to a computer those two categories are totally different. If I sometimes file names under *Refs* and at other times under *References,* I don't have all my important reference contacts available in one place when I need them.

Changing or Reading a Note

I normally write notes because I plan to read them later as reminders. Also, I may need to edit them if the information changes. Opening a note so that you can read it or edit it is simple.

To open a note, follow these steps:

1. If you're not already in the Notes module, click the Notes icon on the Outlook bar.

2. Double-click the title of the note you want to open. It opens! You see the note on your screen.

3. Read the note or make changes as you want.

4. Press Esc to close the note.

If the note you want to read or edit doesn't appear on the screen when you go to the Notes module, *see* the section "Finding a Note," later in this part.

Changing the Color of a Note

The capability to change the color of a note isn't just an aesthetic option. You can assign various colors to different notes and organize your notes in useful ways. I make notes in blue about things I want to include in this book, and I leave all other notes in their normal yellow color.

To assign color to your note, follow these steps:

1. Open the note and click the Note icon in the top-left corner of the note. A shortcut menu appears.

2. Choose C_olor. Another menu appears with a list of colors you can choose.

3. Pick a color. Your note changes to the color you choose.

Choose from blue, green, pink, yellow, or white. You can group or sort your notes according to their color (*see also* "Viewing Notes," later in this part).

Changing the Size of a Note

A note can appear as a teensy little squib, or it can cover your screen. The size of the text in the note is the same no matter how large you make the note. When the note is too small, however, much of your text is invisible, so you have to make the note larger:

1. Click the Notes icon on the Outlook bar, if you're not already in the Notes module.

2. Double-click the title of the note whose size you want to change. The note opens.

3. Move your mouse pointer to the bottom-left corner of the note until the mouse pointer changes into a two-headed arrow pointed on a diagonal.

4. Drag your mouse until the note is the size you want.

In most Windows programs, after you enter more text than will fit in a text box, a scroll bar appears on the right side of the screen. If you want to see text that has scrolled off the bottom of the screen, you click the scroll bar to move the text up. Because notes don't have scroll bars, however, if a note has more text than you can see on the screen, you have to click your mouse on the text and press the arrow keys to scroll up and down through the text. I suppose that those little note boxes are cuter without scroll bars, but they're certainly harder to use.

Creating Notes

If you can click a mouse, you can create a new note:

1. If you're not already in the Notes module, click the Notes icon on the Outlook bar.

2. Click the New icon on the toolbar (or press Ctrl+N). A blank note appears.

3. Enter what you want to say in your note.

4. Press Esc to close and save the note.

Your new note takes its place in the collection of notes in the Notes module. Creating a note doesn't involve a great deal of fuss; just open, type, and close.

 To create a note quickly, you don't even have to switch to the Notes module. Just press Ctrl+Shift+N from any other part of Outlook. A blank note opens, ready for you to fill in. When you've finished writing your note, press Esc to close the note.

Deleting a Note

Creating a huge collection of notes is so easy to do that someday you'll need to delete some of them. Deleting notes is even easier than creating them — it's a piece of cake.

To delete notes, follow these steps:

1. If you're not already in the Notes module, click the Notes icon on the Outlook bar.

2. Click the title of the note you want to delete. The title is highlighted to show which note you've selected.

 3. Click the Delete button on the toolbar (or press Delete). The note disappears.

 You don't have to limit yourself to deleting one note at a time. You can select a bunch of notes by holding down the Ctrl key while clicking the different notes you want to delete; then click the Delete button. You also can click one note and then hold down the Shift key and click another note farther down the row to select both notes you clicked — and all the notes between them. When you click the Delete key, all the notes you selected are deleted.

Finding a Note

After you see how easily you can create a note, you're likely to add notes at your slightest whim, quickly amassing a large collection of notes. Finding one note among a large collection can be a needle-in-a-haystack proposition, except for the Find Items feature. Thank heavens that it's easy to use.

To find items with the Find Items feature, follow these steps:

1. If you're not already in the Notes module, click the Notes icon on the Outlook bar.

2. Click the Find button on the toolbar (or press Alt+I). The Find window opens.

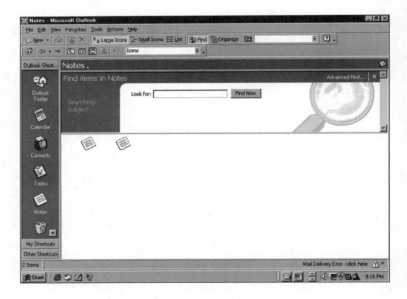

3. In the Look For box, enter the word or phrase you're looking for. It doesn't matter how little text you use for your search. If you're looking for the words *George Washington,* for example, the letters **geo** find any note that contains the words *George Washington.* It also finds *National Geographic* and a reminder to do your geometry homework (assuming that you've written notes about all those things).

4. Click the Find Now button. An hourglass appears as Outlook searches for the text you specified. When Outlook is finished, a list of items that satisfy your search appears.

5. If the note you're looking for turns up, double-click the Note icon to read what the note says. If the note you're looking for doesn't show up, try searching for different text.

6. Click the Find button on the toolbar again (or press Alt+I) to close the Find window.

A nice, weird thing about finding notes is that you don't have to enter a whole word. The Find feature can find any sequence of characters you type. If you're searching for a note you saved about John Paul Kowznofsky, you can search for **John Paul** or just **Kowz.** It doesn't matter whether you use upper- or lowercase letters; Outlook just looks for the letters you entered.

Forwarding a Note to Someone Else

After you've accumulated a treasure trove of information in your collection of notes, you don't need to keep these juicy tidbits to yourself. Forwarding a note to anybody by e-mail is simple.

To forward a note by e-mail, follow these steps:

1. Click the title of the note you want to forward. The title of the note is highlighted.

2. Choose Actions⇨Forward (or press Ctrl+F). The New Message form opens.

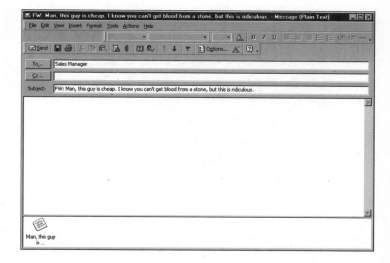

3. Click the To text box and enter the e-mail address of the person to whom you're sending your note. If you want to send a copy to a second person, click the Cc text box and then enter the e-mail addresses of the people to whom you want to send a copy of your note.

4. Enter the subject of the note in the Subject box.

5. If you want, enter the text of a message in the text box.

6. Click the Send button (or press Alt+S). Your message is on its way to your recipient.

What you're really sending is an e-mail message with a note attached, which is very quick and simple but not terribly magical. For the recipient to be able to read the Outlook note, keep in mind that he also needs Outlook.

Printing a List of Your Notes

Printing lists of the notes you've created is a WYSIWYG (*what you see is what you get*) process. Just choose in which view you want to print your notes, and then start printing.

To print a list of notes, follow these steps:

1. Click the Print button on the toolbar (or press Ctrl+P). The Print dialog box opens.

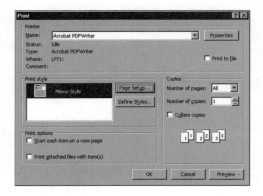

2. Choose Table Style in the Print Style box.

3. Click OK. Your list of notes begins printing.

If you don't want to print all your notes, select the notes you want to print by holding down the Ctrl key and clicking the name of each note you want to print. When you open the Print dialog box, choose Only Selected Rows.

Printing the Contents of a Single Note

Notes are meant to be read on the screen, but now and then I like to print the contents of a note (remember that even though you can change the colors of your notes, the colors don't print on a black-and-white printer):

1. Click the title of the note you want to print. The title of your note is highlighted to show that it was selected.

2. Click the Print button on the toolbar (or press Ctrl+P) to open the Print dialog box.

3. Choose Memo Style in the Print Style box.

4. Click OK. Your note begins printing.

Unfortunately, when you print notes, they don't look like the cute little yellow squares you see on the screen; each one looks like an office memorandum. Maybe the next version of Outlook will make the notes you print look as cute as the notes you see on the screen.

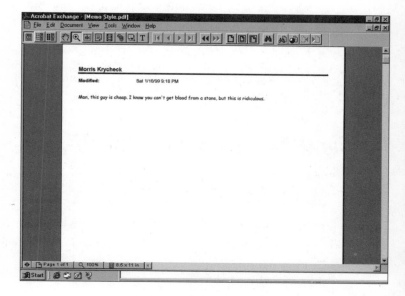

Setting the Default Color and Size of Your Notes

Maybe yellow just isn't your color. Maybe you want a little more space when you create a new note. You can set up Outlook to start each note in the color and size you want (within reason).

To change the default settings for the color and size of your notes, follow these steps:

1. Choose Tools⇨Options. The Options dialog box opens.

2. Click the Note Options button. The Notes Options dialog box appears.

3. Click the scroll-down button at the right end of the Color box.

4. Choose a color from the list that appears.

5. Click the scroll-down button at the right end of the Size box.

6. Click OK.

Changing the default size and color of your notes has no effect on the notes you've already created. If you want to change the color of a note after you've created it, just open the note and change the color (*see also* "Changing the Color of a Note," earlier in this part).

Turning Off the Date-and-Time Display

When you first start Outlook, each note you create includes on the note's bottom line the time and date you created the note. If that doesn't suit you, you can exclude the time and date information.

To turn off the date-and-time display, follow these steps:

1. Choose Tools⇨Options. The Options dialog box appears.

2. Click the Other tab to open the Other options page.

3. Click the Advanced Options button to open the Advanced Options dialog box.

4. Click the When Viewing <u>N</u>otes, Show Time and Date check box to remove the check mark.

5. Click OK to close the Advanced Options dialog box.

6. Click OK to close the Options dialog box.

Even if you turn off the time-and-date display, Outlook displays the time and date of each note's creation in every view except for Icons view (*see also* the following section, "Viewing Notes"). Changing the date-and-time setting changes only what appears on the little yellow (or blue or green or whatever) square.

Viewing Notes

You can make Outlook display your multitude of notes in a variety of ways. Each type of screen style, called a *view,* emphasizes something different about your collection of notes. You can change between the different views of your notes by choosing <u>V</u>iew⇨ Current <u>V</u>iew and picking a different view. You can choose from the following views:

✦ **Icons:** Splashes your collection of notes in little boxes all over the screen. To open one, just click the box representing the note you want to open.

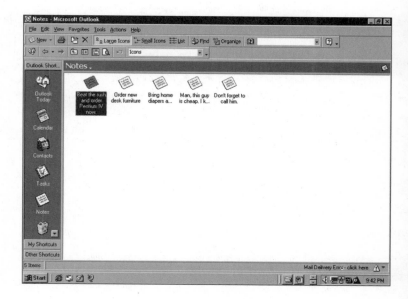

✦ **Notes List:** As its name suggests, presents a two-column list of your notes. One column is for the subject of each note, and the other column is for the date on which you created each note. You can sort the list according to the date you created each note by clicking the word *Created* in the gray box at the top of the column. You also can sort the list in alphabetical order by subject by clicking the word *Subject* in the gray box at the top of the column.

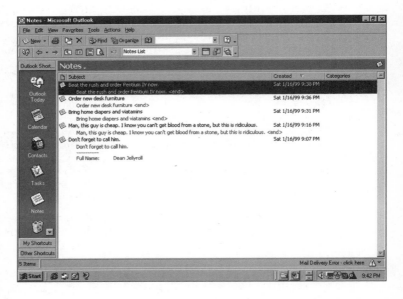

✦ **Last Seven Days:** Shows only notes you've modified within the past seven days. After more than seven days have passed since you changed either the text in a note or its color, size, or category, the note disappears from Last Seven Days view, although you see notes of all ages in all other views.

✦ **By Category:** Groups your notes according to the category you've assigned to each one.

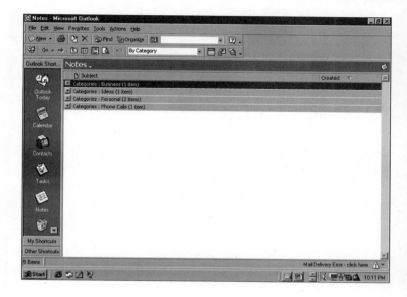

✦ **By Color:** Groups your notes according to the color you've assigned to each one (*see also* "Changing the Color of a Note," earlier in this part).

Part VIII

Files and Folders

Keeping track of the files and folders you create with Office 2000 is an important task. The tools Outlook provides makes keeping track a bit easier. If you've always avoided dealing with files and folders, you may find the whole process less confusing when you're using Outlook. If you're already a file-management expert, you'll appreciate the new features you get with Outlook.

In this part . . .

✔ **Basics of files and folders**

✔ **Managing your files and folders**

✔ **Printing and viewing files and folders**

✔ **Some quick tricks**

Basics of Files and Folders

Although some computer smartypants like to use strange terms, like *files* and *folders* (or *paths*), to make themselves sound smart, the ideas are rather simple. I give you the most basic basics here. If you want more, get a copy of *Windows 95 For Dummies,* 2nd Edition, by Andy Rathbone (IDG Books Worldwide, Inc.) for the entire lowdown on computer file-management concepts.

About files, folders, and drives

The basic elements of organization on the computer are files, folders, and drives:

✦ *Files* are the things you create with your word processor, spreadsheet, and other programs. Whether you call them Letters to Mom or Monthly Report, both are just files to your computer. Files can have different sizes, measured in K (for kilobytes, or thousands of bytes). The 2-page letter you wrote to Mom is probably a smaller file than the 50-page sales report you create at work.

✦ *Folders* are places you create for storing your precious files. Imagine each of the files you create with your word processor as a document, and imagine the folder as the file folder in which you store a group of documents.

✦ *Disk drives* are like the filing cabinets in which you store all the files and folders. A floppy disk (sometimes called diskette) is like a small filing cabinet, big enough to hold maybe a thousand documents, in or out of folders. Floppy disk drives are usually called drive A these days. You also have a disk drive built into your computer, usually called drive C, which acts just like your drive A, except that it's much bigger — big enough to hold hundreds of thousands of documents and the folders you put them in.

Although network drives work just like hard disk drives, they're not built into your computer. Though they're named similarly — with letters (like drive F, G, or Z) — network drives are located on another computer on the network to which your computer is connected. If you're not connected to a network, you don't have any network drives.

Looking at drives

You can see, through My Computer, your entire collection of disk drives and the files that fill them. You also have a My Computer icon on your Windows desktop. You can look at your collection of files and folders in a greater variety of views by using Outlook than by using the regular Windows My Computer icon.

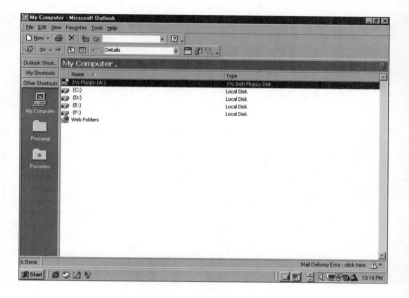

To survey your collection of drives, click the Other Shortcuts group on the Outlook bar and then click the My Computer icon. The Outlook screen shows a list of all the disk drives available to you. If your computer is connected to a network, a list of all the available network drives appears. If you're using a stand-alone computer, you see only the drives on your own computer, probably disk drive A and the hard drive, drive C.

Looking at folder lists

Disk drives, especially hard drives and network drives, are normally chock-full of folders. Although folders seem like a distraction at first, they're really a big help. Imagine a filing cabinet big enough to hold 10,000 documents filled to the brim with no file folders to help organize the contents of the cabinet. No one could ever find anything in a mess like that. A nice, neat collection of file folders makes the biggest collection of files easier to use.

To see the folders you have, follow these steps:

1. Click the My Computer icon on the Outlook bar. A list of your disk drives appears on the screen.

2. Double-click the icon for drive C (or whatever drive you want to view) to reveal the list of folders on the drive.

Remember that if you click the icon for the disk drive, drive A, you have to be sure that a disk is in the drive. If you ask your computer to show you the contents of a disk that isn't there, you can expect a very long pause followed by an error message saying that the drive is not ready.

Also remember that you can have folders inside folders. If you're looking for a specific folder on your disk drive, it may be inside another folder. If at first you don't see the folder you're seeking, open the folder that you think contains your folder, by double-clicking the first folder's icon. The list of items in the folder you opened includes folders that are inside your first folder. (Got that?)

Looking at lists of your files

Files contain the nitty-gritty, nuts-and-bolts information you use. Every document you create is stored as a file somewhere in your computer. Office 2000 likes to send all the files it creates to the My Documents folder, although other programs can send their files wherever they want, so you may have to hunt around to find a file you need.

To look at your files, follow these steps:

1. Click the My Computer icon on the Outlook bar. A list of your drives appears.

2. Double-click the icon for drive C (or whatever drive you want to view). You see a list of the contents of drive C — a collection of folders and files.

3. Double-click the icon for the My Documents folder (or whatever folder you want to look in). The My Documents folder opens and reveals a list of the files and folders it contains. You can also access the My Documents folder directly from the Outlook bar, just beneath the My Computer icon.

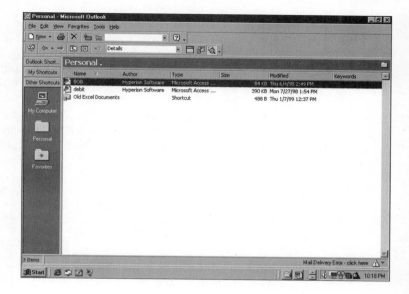

Your list of files may show you more information about each file than you really want to know, such as its size, type, and the last date the file was modified. Don't worry; if you're using Outlook to view your files, you can customize the screen to show you as much or as little information as you want. You can rearrange views of your files in Outlook exactly the way you can rearrange views of any other group of items (*see also* "Rearranging views," in Part V).

Managing Files and Folders

Every time you start a program on your computer, you create, change, or move a file. After you create enough files, you may have to delete or move older files to make room for the new ones. You also may want to delete some files to reduce clutter on your computer and find more easily the files you need. Now and then, you may have to exchange files with other people by e-mail, so you need a good set of tools for finding and dealing with the files you're exchanging. Outlook has all the tools you need for your daily file-management tasks.

Choosing files

If you've already used any Windows program, you're used to the idea of selecting — clicking an item with your mouse to tell Windows that you plan to do something to or with that item. After selecting an item, you can cut, copy, format, move, open, rename, or do heaven-knows-what to the item you've selected.

Files work in exactly the same way. If you plan to do something to a file, such as move or copy the file, you find the file and click the filename to select it. If you want to do something to several files at one time, you have more choices:

+ **Select multiple files, all in a row:** Click one file to select that file, and then hold down the Shift key and click (called a *Shift+click*) another file several rows above or below the first file you selected. When you Shift+click the second file, both files you clicked are selected, along with all the files in between.

+ **Select multiple files, not in a row:** Click one file to select that file, and then hold down the Ctrl key while clicking the other files you want to select. Even if the files you click aren't located next to each other, all the files you *Ctrl+click* are selected.

Copying and moving files

The main reason you have a My Computer icon in Outlook is to enable you to move or copy files between different folders or drives. When you click the icon for any other Outlook module, you see a list of items in that module; you see your contacts when you click the Contacts icon, for example, and your tasks when you click the Tasks icon. Clicking the My Computer icon shows you files and folders on your computer.

To move a file from one folder to another, follow these steps:

1. Click the My Computer icon on the Outlook bar. A list of your drives appears.

2. Double-click the icon for drive C (or whatever drive you want to view). You see a list of the contents of that drive — a collection of folders and files.

3. Double-click the icon for the My Documents folder (or what- ever folder you want to look in). The My Documents folder opens and reveals a list of the files and folders it contains.

4. Select the file (or files) you want to move. The files you click are highlighted to show that you've selected them.

5. Drag the file to the folder to which you want it to move.

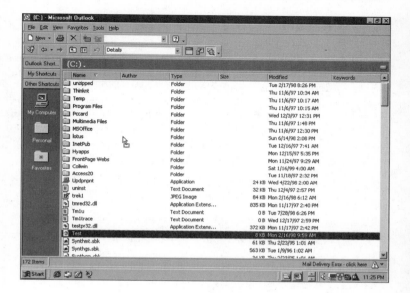

If the folder to which you drag the file is on the same drive (such as drive C) as the folder from which you dragged it, the file is moved. If you press and hold down the Ctrl key while dragging the file, the file is *copied*. If you drag the file to a different drive, the file is copied unless you hold down the Shift key while dragging the file; then the file is moved.

Deleting files

Another good reason to go to the My Computer section is to delete files you don't need anymore. Old, unused files don't wither and mold like leftovers in the fridge; rather, they sit around and waste precious space. Because your disk drive fills up surprisingly quickly, you have to dump unused files now and then. Fortunately, deleting files is easy.

To delete files, follow these steps:

1. Select the file (or files) you want to delete. The file is high-lighted to show that you've selected it.

 2. Click the Delete button on the toolbar (or press Delete).

3. When the dialog box appears and asks whether you're sure, click Yes. Your file disappears.

If you want to clear out bunches of files, select several files at one time (***see also*** "Choosing files," earlier in this part).

Renaming files

You can rename files to help you remember what's in them. If you
previously used DOS or Windows 3.1, you were limited to eight-
character filenames; therefore, you had to name your Annual Sales
Report something like **AnSlsRpt**. With Windows, however, you can
use as many as 255 characters for filenames. So now you can call
the Annual Sales Report something clever, like **Annual Sales
Report.** Now that it's so easy, you may want to go back and rename
all your files so that they have names that make sense to you.

To rename files, follow these steps:

1. Right-click the name of the file you want to rename to open
the shortcut menu.

2. Choose Rename from the menu to open the Rename dialog box.

3. Type the new name of the file in the Rename dialog box.

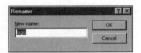

4. Click OK. Your new filename appears.

 Before you go hog-wild renaming all your files, remember that
older programs still understand only the old eight-letter scheme.
If you rename a file that you need to use in an older program, you
see names like Annual~1.txt when you try to open the file in the
older program. If you use only programs written after 1996, you
see the long filenames.

Renaming folders

Folders exist to make it easier for you to find your files. Also, some
programs have their own folders all to themselves and keep the
files they create close to home. Folders have names the program
gives them or names you give them.

Now and then, you may need to rename a folder. If you keep a
folder named This Year's Taxes, for example, someday you may
rename the folder Last Year's Taxes. (Better yet, include the actual
year, or else you may need to have Year-Before-Last-Year's Taxes
and Year Before the Year-Before-Last-Year's Taxes — soon you'll be
awash in Years Before.)

Follow these steps to rename a folder:

1. Right-click the name of the folder you want to rename to open
the shortcut menu.

2. Choose Rename from the shortcut menu. The Rename dialog box appears.

3. Type the new name of the folder in the Rename dialog box.

4. Click OK. Your new folder name appears.

Don't rename the following two folders: *My Documents* is the folder where most Windows programs look to find the documents you've created. Although you can tell your programs to look elsewhere, why go to the trouble? Your *Windows* folder also is very important; if you rename the Windows folder, your computer probably won't start, so leave it alone.

Printing and Viewing Files and Folders

You can use Outlook to print or view lists of the names of all your files, along with details about each file, such as the age of each file, its size, and the name of the program that created the file. If you have a program named QuickView installed, you also can print or view the contents of any file. Although QuickView is included with Windows, it isn't installed unless you make a point of it.

Get a copy of *Windows 95 For Dummies,* 2nd Edition, by Andy Rathbone (IDG Books Worldwide, Inc.), for more information about QuickView.

About views

In all the other modules of Outlook, you view items. *Items* are just small units of information that Outlook uses to organize all the stuff you enter every day. To some extent, Outlook items are figments of Outlook's imagination; no other program can see Outlook items. When you go over to the My Computer module, you're dealing with files — the actual units of information that other programs have created. Outlook shows you the files created by Word, Excel, and any other program you use, like Bozo's Clown Drawing program or anything you may have downloaded from the Internet.

In this section, I use the word *viewing* to mean looking at lists of the names of your files and the details associated with each file (*see also* "About views" in Part V). If you want to view the contents of a file, right-click the name of the file and then choose QuickView from the shortcut menu.

Choosing a view

You can slice and dice lists of information about your files in literally hundreds of different ways when you're using Outlook. The half-dozen predefined views that come installed when you first use Outlook give you a good selection. You can choose any view of your files by choosing View➪Current View and picking the view you want:

+ **Icons:** Spreads a bunch of icons all over the screen, each representing one file. The icons you see differ, depending on the type of file you're seeing. Files created by Microsoft Word have a different type of icon than files created by Excel, which are different from the icons that represent Quicken files, for example.

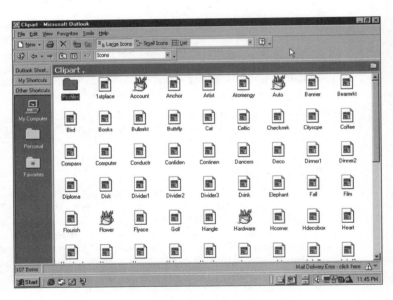

+ **Details:** Shows you a simple list of your files by name, along with the size of each file, the last date you modified the file, and the author of the file (if author information is available).

+ **By Author:** Groups your files according to the author of each file. Because not every program you use keeps track of the author of each file, many files may end up under a group named None.

Office 2000 programs track the name of the author of each document; if you use only Office 2000 programs, Author view may be useful to you.

✦ **By File Type:** Groups your files according to type, which really means the name of the program that created the file. You then can view only your word processing files, only your spreadsheet files, or only any other type of file, as you prefer.

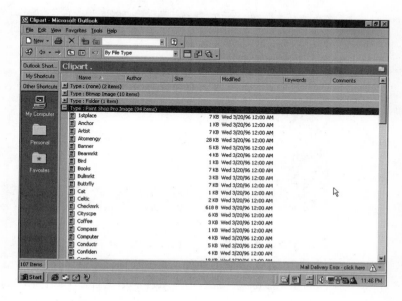

✦ **Document Timeline:** A graph of icons, arranged to show when you worked on each document and for how long. The document timeline is handy for times when you can recall when you worked on a document but not where you filed the document.

✦ **Programs:** Shows program files only — the actual computer programs that do all the work of your computer.

You don't want to delete, move, or rename program files unless you have a good reason for doing so. Programs view, however, makes it easier to find program files when you need them.

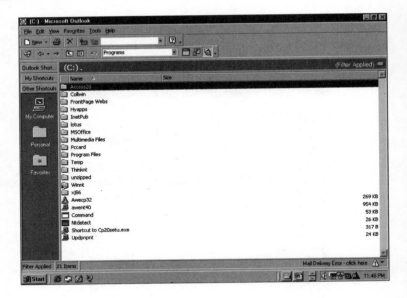

Copying a list of filenames to use in another program

One file-management trick you can do in Outlook that you can't readily do otherwise is to copy a list of filenames and details and then paste the list into another program, such as Microsoft Word or Excel. Using this technique helps you keep track of the progress of projects that involve the creation of many files. For example, while I wrote this book, I wanted to know how many parts were finished, how many illustrations were finished, and other information.

Follow these steps to copy a list of filenames to use in another program:

1. Open the folder in which you stored the files whose names you want to copy (*see also* "Choosing a view," earlier in this part). A list of your files appears.

2. Select the files whose names you want to copy (*see also* "Choosing files," earlier in this part). The files you select are highlighted.

3. Choose Edit⇨Copy (or press Ctrl+C).

4. If the other program is not open, click the Start button and then find and open the program.

5. Choose Edit⇨Paste (or press Ctrl+V) where you want the list to appear. The list of file details appears in the new document.

By pasting a list of file details into a spreadsheet such as Excel, you can calculate total file size, sort the files, or perform any calculation on the information you pasted.

Formatting columns

Column formatting is the term Outlook uses for the type and amount of information that shows up in any column view, as well as what kind of abbreviations Outlook uses to express the information. The best example of column formatting is the way dates are shown. The date and time you modify each file is displayed in the Modified field. If you prefer the most complete version of the date, you can have Outlook display the date as Wednesday, March 4, 1999, 12:15 PM. If you want the date to look more concise, you can choose to show the date in the shortest way possible, as 3/4/99.

To choose how the date and time appear, follow these steps:

1. Open the shortcut menu by right-clicking the title of the column you want to format.

2. Choose Format Columns from the shortcut menu. The Format Columns dialog box appears.

3. From the Available Fields list, choose the format you want to use.

4. Click OK. The column you chose now appears in the format you picked.

Whatever format you choose applies to only the folder you're viewing. If you change the date format for the My Documents folder and then want to do the same in your Favorites folder, you must switch to the Favorites folder and repeat the process. Folder columns keep the formatting you assign to them until you change them.

Printing a list of files

Printing lists of files is another trick that's hard to do without Outlook. You have many reasons to print a list of a folder's files. Again, my favorite reason is to be able to keep track of my progress when I'm working on projects that involve creating lots of files.

Follow these steps to print a list of files:

1. Open a folder that contains files (*see also* "Looking at lists of your files," earlier in this part).

2. Select a file or group of files you want to print a list of.

 3. Click the Print button on the toolbar (or press Ctrl+P).

4. Choose Table Style from the Print Style list. Table Style prints a list of your files rather than details about just one file.

5. If you want to print a list of only the files you select, choose Only Selected Rows in the Print Range section.

6. Click OK to start printing your list.

When you click the Print button on the toolbar, Outlook prints the list of your files in whichever view you have on screen. If the view on-screen doesn't include the information you need, switch to a view that does.

Rearranging columns

You can move a column to a new location by simply dragging its heading. You use exactly the same process for rearranging columns in a list of files as you use for rearranging columns in any other Outlook module.

To move the size column next to the name of the file, follow these steps:

1. Choose View⇨Current View⇨Details to see your list of files.

2. Click the Size heading and drag it on top of the Name column. The gray heading box containing the word *Size* moves where you drag it.

3. Release the mouse button.

As you drag the heading across the screen, you see two red arrows moving along the row of remaining column headings. When you release the mouse button, the heading you dragged (in this case, the Size heading) drops into the row of headings specifically in the spot where the arrows point.

Refreshing the list of files

If you are viewing a list of files or folders on a network, a good chance exists that a change can be made to one of them while the list appears on your screen. Because Outlook isn't smart enough to realize that it has happened, you may be viewing files that have been moved or deleted, or the list of folders may not show some that have just been added. To update the list of files and folders shown in Outlook, choose View➪Current Refresh.

Sorting files the quick, simple way

You can sort your list of files in exactly the same way you sort any list of items in other Outlook modules.

To sort files, follow these steps:

1. Choose any view other than Icons view.

2. Click the heading of the column containing the information you want to use to sort your list, such as Name or Date Modified.

Your list of files appears on-screen in order of the type of information in the column you clicked. If you want to reverse the order (from smallest to largest or from largest to smallest), click the heading a second time.

Using grouped views

A *grouped view* organizes your list of files or Outlook items into, yes, *groups* of files. Each group is made up of files that have one similar piece of information, such as the same author or the same program that created each file.

The names of many Outlook views begin with the word *By,* which means that they are grouped views. You can view your files in By Author view or By File Type view. A grouped view clumps the items in the view into groups that have the same piece of information in a certain field. For example, By Type view clumps together all the files of the same type, such as JPEG images.

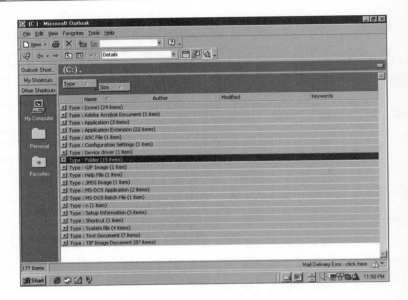

Each group in a grouped view is represented by a gray bar that has a plus or minus sign on the left side. A plus-sign icon tells you that you have more to see in the group. Just click the plus sign to open the group and see which items belong to that group. A minus sign means that the total group is open; you're seeing all there is to see.

Quick Tricks

If you spend lots of time managing files — perhaps because people e-mail files to you or you download lots of files from the Internet or online services — you'll be glad to know that Outlook has some quick tricks for making your lists of files easy to view and for easily navigating around your folders.

Get the best fit

If a column in any view is much wider or narrower than the information in the column, just double-click the line in the gray header row that separates that column from the column to the right. The column width changes to the width of the widest piece of information in the column.

Go up one level

If you spend lots of time putting files in folders, you know that, beneath it all, Windows organizes folders *hierarchically,* which means that all folders are related to each other in the way that branches are related to a tree. Each twig is connected to a branch, and each branch is connected to the trunk; the trunk is connected to the root. If you climb a tree and want to move from one branch to another, one sure way is to move back to the trunk and then to the branch you want. Choosing the Go⇨Up One Level command enables you to move back toward the root and then resume your travel toward the branch you want.

Navigate with browser buttons

Lots of people browse the World Wide Web using browsing programs, such as Netscape and Internet Explorer. Outlook has commands on the Go menu that enable you to browse your computer. When you switch from one folder to another, the browser buttons light up, telling you that they're ready for your use. Suppose that you're copying files from a floppy disk to the My Documents folder; you can easily switch back and forth between two folders by choosing Go⇨Back.

You can also access any of those Web sites you've bookmarked in your Favorites folder. You can access the Favorites folder from the Outlook bar in the same way you access My Computer (click the Other Shortcuts group on the Outlook bar) or from the Go menu to access your list of favorites. Either way, when you select a favorite, Outlook displays the page in your browser, connecting to the Internet first, if necessary.

Techie Talk

ActiveX: A Microsoft technology that stuffs lots of features and functions into little bundles of software. ActiveX enables programs to reuse software that has already been written and supports other programs. ActiveX also makes it easy to distribute little bits of programs, such as downloads from the Internet.

This technology enables computer programs to share information and work with multiple documents at the same time. Outlook is what techies call an *ActiveX container,* which means that you can later add more sophisticated features to the product, as programmers develop things to add. Previously, ActiveX was called OLE (Object Linking and Embedding), although hearing Bill Gates say OLE all the time made people think that he wanted to be a bullfighter.

Address Book: The section of Outlook that stores names and addresses and other information about people you work with every day.

application: A computer program or something that can act like a computer program, responding in various ways to user input.

appointment: An entry in the Calendar module that is assigned to a specific time and date.

archive: A collection of old items put aside for storage.

attachment: A file linked to an e-mail message or other item in Outlook. When you send an e-mail message with a file attached, the recipient of your message receives a copy of the file you attached.

category: A keyword for classifying an item in Outlook. All items can be assigned to one or more categories and sorted or grouped according to the category to which they belong.

contact: An item that includes a person's name, address, and other personal information, which is stored in the Outlook Contacts module.

cool: A term used entirely too often on the Internet, especially to describe authors of computer books.

Date Navigator: The small calendar that turns up in certain views of the Outlook Calendar module that you can use to quickly change the date you're interested in.

directory: The name folders used before they went Big-Time (Windows rather than DOS). See *folder.*

disk drive: The physical device that stores your data. Can be a removable disk (like a disk drive) or a fixed disk (like a hard drive).

drag and drop: A method of moving information within a document or between Outlook modules (and other software programs). To *drag* means to select an object on-screen with the mouse and move the mouse to another area of the screen while holding the mouse button down. To *drop* means to release the mouse button over the part of the screen where you want the object to end up.

e-mail: A system of sending and receiving electronic messages between computers. Messages can include text, pictures, sounds, and computer programs.

event: An item on the Outlook Calendar that happens on a particular date or series of dates but isn't assigned a specific time of the day. Holidays and birthdays are events.

Exchange Server, or Microsoft Exchange Server: A product created by Microsoft to store, transmit, and share messages between groups of computer users. Outlook can be used with Microsoft Exchange Server.

Favorites folder: A folder that stores all your favorite documents and links to sites on the Internet. Clicking the name of an Internet site in your Favorites folder opens your Web browser and connects you to the designated site.

field: A single piece of information in an Outlook item. In a Contact item, for example, a person's name is one field, the job title is another field, the phone number another, and so on. Each item is made up of several fields, which can be displayed as areas on a form or as columns in a list.

file: A named unit of information on your disk. A document can be a file and so can a computer program or a picture or sound.

filter: A way to display only items that satisfy certain criteria and hide all other items. For example, you can filter your Task list to show only the tasks that are due in the next seven days and hide the tasks that are due later.

flag: A setting you can apply to an e-mail message to remind yourself to take action on the message at a specific time. Flagging can also be applied to messages you send to other Outlook users to remind them to take action on the message (that's called *nagging*).

folder: A place where you can store files and other folders. Formerly known as *directories*.

font: A typeface, such as Courier or Times New Roman.

form: A box of information organized to enable you to enter, read, or edit information about a single item. Every time you open an item in Outlook, you see a form that organizes your data.

format: The arrangement of words and numbers in a field. Date formats include simple formats, such as *1/23/98,* or more detailed formats, such as *Tuesday, March 3, 1998.*

group: To organize items into collections that have at least one field containing the same information. To group By Category in Outlook is to gather together items assigned to the same category.

Internet: The network of networks; a collection of computer networks that links other computer networks around the world. Includes the World Wide Web, newsgroups, e-mail, and other attractions that can consume most of your time.

ISP (Internet Service Provider): A firm that connects individual computers and small networks to the Internet. Many online services, such as CompuServe, also function as Internet Service Providers.

Journal: The Outlook module that keeps track of your computer's activities in Outlook and saves information about your activities in a chronological context.

link: A reference to a file in another file. Linked files can share data or enable the viewer to switch between linked files by using a mouse to click the reference to the link.

mail merge: The process of creating a group of letters by combining a single letter with a list of names of the people to whom the letter is to be addressed. When mail-merged letters are sent too often or to the wrong people, they're called *junk mail.*

mailbox: The file that stores all items in Microsoft Outlook or Microsoft Exchange Server. You can have more than one mailbox. (It's not really a box; it's just the name of the file.)

My Computer: The name of the folder that contains all the resources available on a computer running Windows. Resources includes disk drives, folders, network connections, and other devices.

network: A collection of computers that are connected to talk to each other. Computers on a network can share programs and documents and can exchange e-mail.

Notes: The Outlook module that enables you to enter free-form text in the form of colored notes on-screen.

PowerPoint: The graphics presentation program that's part of Office 2000.

preview: A short sample of the first few lines of text in a message or other Outlook item.

properties: The qualities or attributes of a file or other object in Windows. The font is a property of a piece of text; the filename is a property of a file.

recurrence: The pattern by which an appointment or task repeats itself. A recurring appointment happens over and over in a predictable pattern.

regeneration: The pattern by which a task becomes due again a certain amount of time after it was completed the last time.

Registry: A database in Windows that keeps track of all programs and resources on the machine that runs that particular copy of Windows.

Rules Wizard: A program that automatically moves e-mail messages from certain people to a certain folder or deletes e-mail with certain words in the subject line. The Rules Wizard also enables you to make certain things happen when certain kinds of messages arrive, such as playing a rude sound when messages arrive that contain the word *taxes* or making a message pop up on-screen when a high-priority message arrives.

scroll-down button: A triangle at the end of a drop-down list that, when clicked, causes the contents of the list to be revealed so that you can choose an item from the list.

select: To highlight something so that Windows knows that you want to do something to it, such as copy, print, open, or rename. The easiest way to select something is to click it with your mouse or click it and then drag your mouse across it.

server: One computer on a network that holds programs or files for all the other computers on that network to use.

shortcut: An icon in Windows that represents a program, folder, or document located someplace else on the computer. A shortcut enables you to open programs and documents without having to worry about where they're located on the computer.

sort: To organize a list in order. You can use Outlook to sort names alphabetically or to sort other items by date or size. Outlook can't sort the socks in the laundry basket just yet, though.

Start button: The handy little button at the bottom of your Windows screen that you use to start programs, open documents, and find things on your computer.

task: An item of work you need to do that you enter in your Task list so that you'll remember to do it.

taskbar: The stripe across the bottom of the Windows screen that shows you which programs are running. The taskbar also includes tidbits such as the current time and the Start button.

template: An item you use as a pattern for creating other items. You can use templates in Outlook to create e-mail messages that contain information you use over and over, such as a "While you were out" phone message template.

timeline: A graph that displays a collection of documents or Outlook items according to the time you created or scheduled each item.

URL (Uniform Resource Locator): A fancy name for the address of anything on the Internet, especially the World Wide Web, such as http:\\www.dummies.com or any of the www.something.com addresses that have sprouted up everywhere.

view: An arrangement of items in Outlook that you can save and name for later use. Different views help you do different kinds of work. One view of your tasks, for example, shows the tasks you still have to do so that you can get them done; another view shows the tasks you've finished so that you can approach your boss for that raise.

Visual Basic: The programming language that enables people to automate some Office 2000 tasks, especially in Outlook, as well as to do things they haven't thought of yet.

wizard: A series of dialog boxes that guide you step-by-step through procedures that wouldn't make sense to a normal person without help. Wizards can help you create Inbox rules, get remote e-mail, and create a form letter with mail merge.

Word: The word-processing program that accompanies Outlook in the Office 2000 suite. You can use Word 2000 to create fancy-looking e-mail and then send the mail with Outlook to impress your friends. You also can include addresses from your Contact list in Word documents.

World Wide Web: The component of the Internet that delivers information in the form of screens of information connected by links to another. The screens, commonly referred to as *pages,* can contain text, colorful graphics, sound, video clips, and other information. You view these pages on the world Wide Web by using a Web browser, such as Netscape Navigator or Microsoft Internet Explorer. Each Web page has an address (see *URL*) you can enter in any Outlook item.

Index

T

Notes

- Office Excel KeyCode

F4M6 K 8DKPG

QQ8CK 76XQ6

Notes WF7WM

(XP Code)

Notes

Notes

Notes

Notes

_____
_____
_____
_____
_____
_____
_____
_____
_____
_____
_____
_____
_____
_____
_____
_____
_____
_____
_____
_____
_____
_____
_____
_____

Notes

Notes

Notes

Notes

Notes

Notes

Dummies Books™
Bestsellers on Every Topic!

🤓 GENERAL INTEREST TITLES

BUSINESS & PERSONAL FINANCE

Title	Author	ISBN	Price
Accounting For Dummies®	John A. Tracy, CPA	0-7645-5014-4	$19.99 US/$27.99 CAN
Business Plans For Dummies®	Paul Tiffany, Ph.D. & Steven D. Peterson, Ph.D.	1-56884-868-4	$19.99 US/$27.99 CAN
Business Writing For Dummies®	Sheryl Lindsell-Roberts	0-7645-5134-5	$16.99 US/$27.99 CAN
Consulting For Dummies®	Bob Nelson & Peter Economy	0-7645-5034-9	$19.99 US/$27.99 CAN
Customer Service For Dummies®, 2ⁿᵈ Edition	Karen Leland & Keith Bailey	0-7645-5209-0	$19.99 US/$27.99 CAN
Franchising For Dummies®	Dave Thomas & Michael Seid	0-7645-5160-4	$19.99 US/$27.99 CAN
Getting Results For Dummies®	Mark H. McCormack	0-7645-5205-8	$19.99 US/$27.99 CAN
Home Buying For Dummies®	Eric Tyson, MBA & Ray Brown	1-56884-385-2	$16.99 US/$24.99 CAN
House Selling For Dummies®	Eric Tyson, MBA & Ray Brown	0-7645-5038-1	$16.99 US/$24.99 CAN
Human Resources Kit For Dummies®	Max Messmer	0-7645-5131-0	$19.99 US/$27.99 CAN
Investing For Dummies®, 2ⁿᵈ Edition	Eric Tyson, MBA	0-7645-5162-0	$19.99 US/$27.99 CAN
Law For Dummies®	John Ventura	1-56884-860-9	$19.99 US/$27.99 CAN
Leadership For Dummies®	Marshall Loeb & Steven Kindel	0-7645-5176-0	$19.99 US/$27.99 CAN
Managing For Dummies®	Bob Nelson & Peter Economy	1-56884-858-7	$19.99 US/$27.99 CAN
Marketing For Dummies®	Alexander Hiam	1-56884-699-1	$19.99 US/$27.99 CAN
Mutual Funds For Dummies®, 2ⁿᵈ Edition	Eric Tyson, MBA	0-7645-5112-4	$19.99 US/$27.99 CAN
Negotiating For Dummies®	Michael C. Donaldson & Mimi Donaldson	1-56884-867-6	$19.99 US/$27.99 CAN
Personal Finance For Dummies®, 2ⁿᵈ Edition	Eric Tyson, MBA	0-7645-5013-6	$19.99 US/$27.99 CAN
Personal Finance For Dummies® For Canadians	Eric Tyson, MBA & Tony Martin	1-56884-378-X	$19.99 US/$27.99 CAN
Public Speaking For Dummies®	Malcolm Kushner	0-7645-5159-0	$16.99 US/$24.99 CAN
Sales Closing For Dummies®	Tom Hopkins	0-7645-5063-2	$14.99 US/$21.99 CAN
Sales Prospecting For Dummies®	Tom Hopkins	0-7645-5066-7	$14.99 US/$21.99 CAN
Selling For Dummies®	Tom Hopkins	1-56884-389-5	$16.99 US/$24.99 CAN
Small Business For Dummies®	Eric Tyson, MBA & Jim Schell	0-7645-5094-2	$19.99 US/$27.99 CAN
Small Business Kit For Dummies®	Richard D. Harroch	0-7645-5093-4	$24.99 US/$34.99 CAN
Taxes 2000 For Dummies®	Eric Tyson & David J. Silverman	0-7645-5206-6	$14.99 US/$21.99 CAN
Time Management For Dummies®, 2ⁿᵈ Edition	Jeffrey J. Mayer	0-7645-5145-0	$19.99 US/$27.99 CAN
Writing Business Letters For Dummies®	Sheryl Lindsell-Roberts	0-7645-5207-4	$16.99 US/$24.99 CAN

TECHNOLOGY TITLES 🤓

INTERNET/ONLINE

Title	Author	ISBN	Price
America Online® For Dummies®, 5ᵗʰ Edition	John Kaufeld	0-7645-0502-5	$19.99 US/$27.99 CAN
Banking Online Dummies®	Paul Murphy	0-7645-0458-4	$24.99 US/$34.99 CAN
eBay™ For Dummies®	Roland Warner	0-7645-0582-3	$19.99 US/$27.99 CAN
E-Mail For Dummies®, 2ⁿᵈ Edition	John R. Levine, Carol Baroudi, & Arnold Reinhold	0-7645-0131-3	$24.99 US/$34.99 CAN
Genealogy Online For Dummies®	Matthew L. Helm & April Leah Helm	0-7645-0377-4	$24.99 US/$34.99 CAN
Internet Directory For Dummies®, 3ʳᵈ Edition	Brad Hill	0-7645-0558-2	$24.99 US/$34.99 CAN
Internet Auctions For Dummies®	Greg Holden	0-7645-0578-9	$24.99 US/$34.99 CAN
Internet Explorer 5 For Windows® For Dummies®	Doug Lowe	0-7645-0455-X	$19.99 US/$28.99 CAN
Investing Online For Dummies®	Kathleen Sindell, Ph.D,	0-7645-0509-X	$24.99 US/$34.99 CAN
Job Searching Online For Dummies®	Pam Dixon	0-7645-0673-0	$24.99 US/$34.99 CAN
Investing Online For Dummies®, 2ⁿᵈ Edition	Kathleen Sindell, Ph.D.	0-7645-0509-2	$24.99 US/$34.99 CAN
Travel Planning Online For Dummies®, 2ⁿᵈ Edition	Noah Vadnai	0-7645-0438-X	$24.99 US/$34.99 CAN
World Wide Web Searching For Dummies®, 2ⁿᵈ Ed.	Brad Hill	0-7645-0264-6	$24.99 US/$34.99 CAN
Yahoo!® For Dummies®	Brad Hill	0-7645-0582-3	$19.99 US/$27.99 CAN

OPERATING SYSTEMS

Title	Author	ISBN	Price
DOS For Dummies®, 3ʳᵈ Edition	Dan Gookin	0-7645-0361-8	$19.99 US/$27.99 CAN
GNOME For Linux® For Dummies®	David B. Busch	0-7645-0650-1	$24.99 US/$37.99 CAN
LINUX® For Dummies®, 2ⁿᵈ Edition	John Hall, Craig Witherspoon, & Coletta Witherspoon	0-7645-0421-5	$24.99 US/$34.99 CAN
Mac® OS 8.5 For Dummies®	Bob LeVitus	0-7645-0397-9	$19.99 US/$28.99 CAN
Red Hat® Linux® For Dummies®	Jon "maddog" Hall	0-7645-0663-3	$24.99 US/$37.99 CAN
Small Business Windows® 98 For Dummies®	Stephen Nelson	0-7645-0425-8	$24.99 US/$34.99 CAN
UNIX® For Dummies®, 4ᵗʰ Edition	John R. Levine & Margaret Levine Young	0-7645-0419-3	$19.99 US/$27.99 CAN
Windows® 95 For Dummies®, 2ⁿᵈ Edition	Andy Rathbone	0-7645-0180-1	$19.99 US/$27.99 CAN
Windows® 98 For Dummies®	Andy Rathbone	0-7645-0261-3	$19.99 US/$27.99 CAN
Windows® 2000 For Dummies®	Andy Rathbone	0-7645-0641-2	$19.99 US/$29.99 CAN
Windows® 2000 Server For Dummies®	Ed Tittle	0-7645-0341-3	$24.99 US/$37.99 CAN

Dummies Books™
Bestsellers on Every Topic!

 GENERAL INTEREST TITLES

FOOD & BEVERAGE/ENTERTAINING

Bartending For Dummies®	Ray Foley	0-7645-5051-9	$14.99 US/$21.99 CA
Cooking For Dummies®	Bryan Miller & Marie Rama	0-7645-5002-0	$19.99 US/$27.99 CA
Entertaining For Dummies®	Suzanne Williamson with Linda Smith	0-7645-5027-6	$19.99 US/$27.99 CA
Gourmet Cooking For Dummies®	Charlie Trotter	0-7645-5029-2	$19.99 US/$27.99 CA
Grilling For Dummies®	Marie Rama & John Mariani	0-7645-5076-4	$19.99 US/$27.99 CA
Italian Cooking For Dummies®	Cesare Casella & Jack Bishop	0-7645-5098-5	$19.99 US/$27.99 CA
Mexican Cooking For Dummies®	Mary Sue Miliken & Susan Feniger	0-7645-5169-8	$19.99 US/$27.99 CA
Quick & Healthy Cooking For Dummies®	Lynn Fischer	0-7645-5214-7	$19.99 US/$27.99 CA
Wine For Dummies®, 2nd Edition	Ed McCarthy & Mary Ewing-Mulligan	0-7645-5114-0	$19.99 US/$27.99 CA

SPORTS

Baseball For Dummies®, 2nd Edition	Joe Morgan with Richard Lally	0-7645-5234-1	$19.99 US/$27.99 CA
Golf For Dummies®, 2nd Edition	Gary McCord	0-7645-5146-9	$19.99 US/$27.99 CA
Fly Fishing For Dummies®	Peter Kaminsky	0-7645-5073-X	$19.99 US/$27.99 CA
Football For Dummies®	Howie Long with John Czarnecki	0-7645-5054-3	$19.99 US/$27.99 CA
Hockey For Dummies®	John Davidson with John Steinbreder	0-7645-5045-4	$19.99 US/$27.99 CA
NASCAR For Dummies®	Mark Martin	0-7645-5219-8	$19.99 US/$27.99 CA
Tennis For Dummies®	Patrick McEnroe with Peter Bodo	0-7645-5087-X	$19.99 US/$27.99 CA

HOME & GARDEN

Annuals For Dummies®	Bill Marken & NGA	0-7645-5056-X	$16.99 US/$24.99 CA
Container Gardening For Dummies®	Bill Marken & NGA	0-7645-5057-8	$16.99 US/$24.99 CA
Decks & Patios For Dummies®	Robert J. Beckstrom & NGA	0-7645-5075-6	$16.99 US/$24.99 CA
Flowering Bulbs For Dummies®	Judy Glattstein & NGA	0-7645-5103-5	$16.99 US/$24.99 CA
Gardening For Dummies®, 2nd Edition	Michael MacCaskey & NGA	0-7645-5130-2	$16.99 US/$24.99 CA
Herb Gardening For Dummies®	NGA	0-7645-5200-7	$16.99 US/$24.99 CA
Home Improvement For Dummies®	Gene & Katie Hamilton & the Editors of HouseNet, Inc.	0-7645-5005-5	$19.99 US/$26.99 CA
Houseplants For Dummies®	Larry Hodgson & NGA	0-7645-5102-7	$16.99 US/$24.99 CA
Painting and Wallpapering For Dummies®	Gene Hamilton	0-7645-5150-7	$16.99 US/$24.99 CA
Perennials For Dummies®	Marcia Tatroe & NGA	0-7645-5030-6	$16.99 US/$24.99 CA
Roses For Dummies®, 2nd Edition	Lance Walheim	0-7645-5202-3	$16.99 US/$24.99 CA
Trees and Shrubs For Dummies®	Ann Whitman & NGA	0-7645-5203-1	$16.99 US/$24.99 CA
Vegetable Gardening For Dummies®	Charlie Nardozzi & NGA	0-7645-5129-9	$16.99 US/$24.99 CA

TECHNOLOGY TITLES

WEB DESIGN & PUBLISHING

Active Server Pages For Dummies®, 2nd Edition	Bill Hatfield	0-7645-0603-X	$24.99 US/$37.99 CA
Cold Fusion 4 For Dummies®	Alexis Gutzman	0-7645-0604-8	$24.99 US/$37.99 CA
Creating Web Pages For Dummies®, 4th Edition	Bud Smith & Arthur Bebak	0-7645-0504-1	$24.99 US/$34.99 CA
Dreamweaver™ For Dummies®	Janine Warner	0-7645-0423-1	$24.99 US/$34.99 CA
FrontPage® 2000 For Dummies®	Asha Dornfest	0-7645-0423-1	$24.99 US/$34.99 CA
HTML 4 For Dummies®, 2nd Edition	Ed Tittel & Stephen Nelson James	0-7645-0572-6	$24.99 US/$34.99 CA
Java™ For Dummies®, 2nd Edition	Aaron E. Walsh	0-7645-0140-2	$24.99 US/$34.99 CA
PageMill™ 2 For Dummies®	Deke McClelland & John San Filippo	0-7645-0028-7	$24.99 US/$34.99 CA
XML™ For Dummies®	Ed Tittel	0-7645-0692-7	$24.99 US/$37.99 CA

DESKTOP PUBLISHING GRAPHICS/MULTIMEDIA

Adobe® In Design™ For Dummies®	Deke McClelland	0-7645-0599-8	$19.99 US/$27.99 CA
CorelDRAW™ 9 For Dummies®	Deke McClelland	0-7645-0523-8	$19.99 US/$27.99 CA
Desktop Publishing and Design For Dummies®	Roger C. Parker	1-56884-234-1	$19.99 US/$27.99 CA
Digital Photography For Dummies®, 3rd Edition	Julie Adair King	0-7645-0646-3	$24.99 US/$37.99 CA
Microsoft® Publisher 98 For Dummies®	Jim McCarter	0-7645-0395-2	$19.99 US/$27.99 CA
Visio 2000 For Dummies®	Debbie Walkowski	0-7645-0635-8	$19.99 US/$29.99 CA